Not Just Sunday

Jevon Caldwell-Gross

Not Just Sunday

Reimagine the Reach
and Rhythms of Your Church

Abingdon Press
Nashville

NOT JUST SUNDAY:
REIMAGINE THE REACH AND RHYTHMS OF YOUR CHURCH

ISBN: 9781791038052

Library of Congress Control Number: 2025944845

Book cover of "Not Just Sunday: Reimagine the Reach and Rhythms of Your Church" by Jevon Caldwell-Gross features abstract watercolor figures walking toward a church in the background.

MANUFACTURED IN THE UNITED STATES OF AMERICA

Contents

Acknowledgments

I am deeply grateful for the congregations that have shaped my ministry and helped form the foundation of this book.

To Hamilton Memorial United Methodist Church—thank you for being the first community to trust me as your pastor. Though small in number, we dreamed big and made a meaningful impact together.

To St. Mark's United Methodist Church ("The Mark")—thank you for being a place of innovation and imagination. It was there that we planted seeds, tried new things, and embraced the unknown with courage and hope.

To St. Luke's United Methodist Church—thank you for giving me a platform to lead, grow, and stretch beyond what I imagined possible. Your boldness, excellence, and inclusive spirit inspired much of what is written here.

Each of you left a mark on me and I carry your lessons, your stories, and your faith into this next chapter.

Chapter 1

The Church in a Changed World

If you are reading this book, that means you still believe in the local church. You have not given up on the possibility that God still invites imperfect people to be a part of what God is already doing in the world. Considering the ongoing decline in attendance within mainline denominations and the challenges facing the institutional church, there remains a resilient hope for the future. At times, this seems difficult to embrace. The current political climate has deeply impacted many churches, often creating division within congregations and reshaping how people engage with faith communities. With polarized discourse dominating public life, many churches have found themselves navigating difficult conversations on social justice, national identity, and moral and spiritual authority. Some have leaned into advocacy, while others have struggled to define their role in the presence of differing political perspectives.

In many circles, the church has lost its influence and is no longer seen as a credible voice of authority. It has been branded with themes of irrelevance, judgment, and, for some, oppressive. The stories of church hurt continue to uncover the dysfunction and toxicity that reside within the so-called sacred walls. What God intended to be a place of refuge and belonging has, for some, evolved into a place responsible for unspeakable hurt and exclusion. And yet, God's grace continues to be sufficient.

With its imperfections, there still exists immense possibility. The church has arrived at a critical point in history where it will either continue fading into irrelevance or seize this moment. This goes beyond simply getting people to return to a building. This is not just another chance to replicate the church that once existed or to try harder at what was no longer working. Times are different. The culture has changed. The world as we know it will continue to evolve.

God has uniquely positioned the church to reclaim its voice and fulfil the mission of making disciples for the transformation of the world. However, it will require a new way of approaching ministry and an openness to learning and failing. It will necessitate a fresh approach to ministry and a willingness to learn from both our successes and our failures. It will involve looking beyond the conventional focus of Sunday mornings to connect with new audiences and deepen engagement as individuals progress in their discipleship.

I am writing because I still believe in the church. I believe because I have seen the church at its worst and its best. When we are at our best something divine happens. I have seen the church surround people at their lowest moments and help them discover the true power of redemption. I have seen the church welcome and love individuals that thought they were not worthy of God's love. I witnessed firsthand the church be a place where young people served, led, and even stood before the congregation to express a call to ministry. I have seen the church remind people that second chances were possible. I have seen the church call out injustice and commit to dismantling systems of oppression. I have seen glimpses of the church truly live as the embodiment of Christ in the world.

You are reading this because at one time, you too have seen the church at its best and believe its best days are yet to come. For the majority who found their way to this work, you may find yourself in one of these categories:

Denominational Leaders

If you are a denominational leader in any capacity, you hold a vital responsibility in providing direction, resourcing, and setting goals for the clergy and churches you lead. The way you envision effective ministry, the criteria you choose for evaluation, and the support you offer to congregational leaders are immensely significant to the health and future growth of the church. It's crucial to consider the metrics and data you will use to assess effectiveness and vitality within your congregations. What new or necessary skills are you seeking to foster to help these churches flourish? Are you recruiting leaders equipped to pastor yesterday's church, or are you identifying those who can lead in this new emerging context? Have you considered how the process or experience of ordination or formal church leadership affirms or opposes this reality?

Given the particular challenges many churches face within your denomination and the region you oversee, it's important to recognize that countless congregations continue to struggle with effective ministry in the post-pandemic landscape. Church closures are still on the rise, and worship attendance numbers are still declining. Many churches are grappling with sustainability and find themselves ill-equipped to meet the evolving demands of modern ministry. While some congregations may desire growth, they often don't know where to begin. Others may have become resistant to change, clinging to the traditions of the church they have always known.

As a denominational leader, you play a crucial role in shaping the narrative of this new ministry landscape. You are entrusted with the important task of guiding these congregations and their leaders through a terrain that is not only unfamiliar but is also in a state of constant evolution. Your leadership is instrumental in ensuring that both your leaders and congregational members are equipped with the tools they need to navigate these changes effectively. More importantly, you can help them thrive and fully embrace their unique callings within their communities. By fostering an environment of learning, support, and innovation, you can empower the current and next generation of church leaders to meet the challenges of today's ministry with confidence and competence, setting them up for success.

Clergy or Pastoral Leadership

Whether your ministerial journey began before, during, or after the pandemic, nothing has truly prepared you for this next phase of ministry. Give yourself permission to experience the same grace you have so freely offered to others. (Don't rush past that statement; allow it to resonate with you. Read it again if necessary.) While previous experiences will certainly be helpful, we must embrace on-the-job learning, laying the tracks as we move forward.

For those who have been in ministry before 2020, you may find it challenging to lead in the same manner. Your previous experience or expertise will have its limits. I've seen firsthand the frustration of colleagues trying to navigate and lead a church that no longer exists. It can be emotionally draining to invest years in building something, witness God's expansion of certain aspects of the congregation, and then suddenly realize that the landscape has shifted. Your new strategies and approaches must align with the reality of the church you have today, not the one you once knew. In this new paradigm of ministry, you will be called to name the current reality with honesty, while also casting a clear, Spirit-led vision that invites people to imagine and move toward a future they have not yet experienced, one that is filled with purpose, possibility, and hope.

In this new landscape, one of the greatest gifts you can offer is not merely your expertise or experience, but your willingness to learn, grow, adapt, and listen. In past discussions about church growth, the focus often centered on how to lead change and guide others through it. Now, we must shift our perspective to include ourselves as part of that transformative experience. It's not just about introducing change, but a willingness to embrace it ourselves. Consider expanding your library to include contemporary voices and fresh perspectives. There may be new skills you need to cultivate to effectively reach new audiences. Don't hesitate to embrace the role of a novice; initial discomfort is a part of the learning process. Your leadership will set the tone for your church's ability to change and evolve. The church deeply needs our vulnerability and humility in this journey.

Most importantly, prioritize your mental health; there's a heavy burden on your shoulders. The learning process can be taxing. COVID-19 has already taken its toll, and some may never fully recover. Several of my colleagues have taken sabbaticals, while others are still trying to catch their breath. Yet, amidst all of this, Sundays come every week—sermons need to be preached, needs must be met, hospitals require visits, and programs must be planned. The pace of change continues to accelerate, but none of this will matter if you aren't healthy and fully present. Leading in today's context is undeniably demanding. You deserve to bring your best self, not just for those you serve, but for your own well-being.

View from the Pew

I am intentionally writing this book to include the experiences and influence of the laity. I have read several books on church growth aimed at equipping pastors and clergy, operating under the assumption that congregational leaders would share their insights. I often found myself attending conferences and growth opportunities as if I were a Moses-like figure ascending a mountain, tasked with relaying what I had heard and seen. While that has its place, the most effective experiences occur when pastors and laypeople learn together. This collaboration fosters common language, mutual understanding, and shared ownership of the mission.

Your role is critical. None of this progress happens without you. You are the church that Jesus described. When Jesus called the church to go to the ends of the earth, I am convinced it was not solely a summons to ordained clergy. It was a call to equip all people to step into the world and lead. You lead in your families, workplaces, communities, and relationships, as well as within the walls of the church.

Your collective influence far exceeds the potential of any single pastor or denominational leader. You possess invaluable gifts and perspectives that your church and community desperately need. The visions and dreams you hold for your church depend on your involvement, especially as your church responds to the ever-changing landscape of ministry. There is no hope for the future of the church without your leadership, support, ideas, gifts, and readiness to learn and grow.

This means that you may find yourself serving and leading in different ways. For those who have been connected to your church for an extended period, initial discomfort may arise. The church might look and feel different, especially after experiencing a global pandemic. However, use your voice to remind those around you that God is not done with your church just yet.

So, as we go through this journey, try this: Consider five people in your circle of influence who are going through a difficult time and are not connected to a faith community. (Take a moment to record their names in a place that will be readily visible as you read this book.) We will continue to refer to these names throughout the remaining chapters as our *Five Faces*. Think of a family member, neighbor, schoolmate, close friend, or maybe even an entire family, and imagine what they might be thinking and feeling. Which one of these people needs a fresh start or a second chance? Who needs to be reminded that God still exists, and the church still matters? Reflect on the questions they may be asking and the concerns that might be present. Now, imagine creating a community and faith experience that reminds them of a God who hears, cares, and sees them. Envision a space where they can bring their whole selves and simply "be." Together, we get to envision and create that place.

The Other 164 Hours

At the time of the book's release, I will have fully transitioned into my role as Director of Revitalization and New Church Development for the Indiana Conference of The United Methodist Church, after spending the past seven years on staff at St. Luke's UMC in Indianapolis.

In the year 2020, we set a goal at St. Luke's of reaching 2020 first-time guests in worship. A consultant analyzed our metrics and concluded that to continue growing in worship attendance, there needed to be more attention placed on reaching a higher number of first-time guests.

At the time, I was overseeing our front-facing ministries (Communications, New Here, Hospitality, and Online Community), so I paid special attention to these numbers and follow-up data. Although the target number of first-time guests marked a significant increase from previous years, each ministry within the church developed strategic plans to support and contribute to the overall effort. This became a rallying point for the year. There were plans to celebrate our progress as a staff and congregation to keep the goal in front of us as the year progressed.

Then COVID-19 happened. I remember being called into the office of our Senior Pastor, Rob Fuquay, for an emergency meeting along with several other staff members. The decision to cancel the upcoming worship services were conveyed and we immediately had to pivot. This was not an easy decision. We hosted five worship services, three traditional and two contemporary, every week with programming for kids and students of all ages. We had a choir and orchestra for the traditional services and a full band for the contemporary services. Because some of the services ran concurrently, two preachers were required each week. But within a matter of days, we had to become a different church. Like many other congregations, we had to transition to online services, and our entire process changed. None of us had prepared for this moment. What was supposed to last a few weeks lasted for months, and even years for some congregations. I am convinced that to some extent, every church had to become something different.

One thing that COVID-19 did not change for us was our goals. We stayed committed to the goal of reaching our targeted number of new guests despite the hard shift from our ministry programming and worship services. While our services and selected programming remained virtual, our congregational surveys revealed that people managed to stay engaged within the life of the church. What was most surprising was the rising number of first-time guests.

I noticed a significant trend indicating a shift in how we engaged with these new guests. In the past, we primarily focused on attendance data gathered on Sunday mornings. We had a dedicated ministry that based its follow-up procedures on the number of people who recorded their attendance during the worship service. Prior to COVID-19, we would distribute sign-in booklets throughout the pews to encourage attendees to record their attendance. However, as we analyzed the data, it became clear that a different trend was emerging. While fewer people were signing in during our online services, we were still meeting our engagement goals with new guests, but through different channels than we had anticipated.

For instance, we hosted an anti-racism training seminar for our church and community, and a significant number of first-time guests registered and attended this event. It was an unforeseen, but prevalent need in our community, thus attracting people from various industries and professions. Our congregation had built enough credibility and trust that our community was willing to listen and depend on us to fill that void. As a supplement to this training, we introduced community-wide small groups based on Austin Channing Brown's book, *I'm Still Here: Black Dignity in a World Made for Whiteness*. Again, we saw a considerable number of new registrations from persons not connected to our faith community. With similar events, the number of new guests in 2020 totaled 2,300, far exceeding our goal!

This all occurred in a year when much of our regular programming was suspended, and we mostly worshipped online. New people were connecting with the church, but Sunday morning was no longer the central place where this was happening or being recorded. A large majority of those new persons were finding connections to the congregations outside of the Sunday morning worship experience. Sunday was a day, but it was no longer *the* day. The numbers were signaling a shift in the ways that people were engaging faith and revealing the possibilities outside of Sunday morning.

Like many congregations, the numbers challenged our approach. For us and many churches, Sunday is a major day in the life of the church. Sunday is sacred. It's how many churches track and gauge their growth and ability to connect with the community. Consider how much labor and time is required to provide an engaging experience every single week. There is rehearsal time needed for musicians and singers. The pastor or preacher spends hours researching and crafting sermons. Children's and student ministries prepare lessons, crafts, or games that will engage their youth. Bulletins or worship guides are printed. Volunteers must be scheduled to perform a variety of jobs. Depending on the size of your church, there are a host of other staff members who must be present on a Sunday morning. I have served in a variety of contexts and in various-sized churches. I have served in congregations where our staff only consisted of myself, a musician, and a secretary. And yet, in every single context, Sunday was always important. There was no other experience in the church that required this amount of consistent labor and resources. And as a colleague told me when I first started pastoring, "Sunday comes quick . . . and often!"

And yet, the numbers told a fuller picture of the possibilities that were present. It marked a shift in our community. Sunday was a day, but not the only day when our community connected with our congregation. We place much of our efforts on one day of the week, in a limited window between 8:00 a.m. and 12:00 p.m. We judge our effectiveness by what happens in a small four-hour window that occurs one day a week. We plan, we invest, we train, we think through every single element. And yet, most churches don't apply that same level of labor and intentionality to the other 164 hours of the week. We don't apply that same intentionality to the time and places where people are actually gathering. Our greatest potential to impact our communities, reach new audiences, and provide opportunities for further engagement can't be limited to one day of the week, but must include how we approach the other 164 hours of the week.

Beyond Sunday

When my role took another shift to provide more leadership and direction as our Online Community Pastor, I began consulting with various churches, facilitating workshops and seminars across denominations, and teaching practical theology courses around hybrid ministry. The more I connected with various pastors in different settings and coached leadership teams, the more I saw common themes emerging. It was clear that many churches were simply trying to "get back to normal" or strategizing around convincing their members to return to church. There was a consistent struggle over how to meaningfully engage those who worshipped online and provide meaningful in-person experiences. Leaders struggled strategically and theologically. Most had never truly taken the opportunity to reflect, retreat, and regather because of the weekly demands of Sunday morning. Therefore, most simply returned to their regularly scheduled programming. Churches wanted to grow and reengage their members, but didn't have the necessary skills or knowledge to do this effectively in this new ministry landscape. The desire was present, but the approach was absent.

The aim of this book is not to diminish the quality or time devoted to your worship experience. It is, however, an invitation to plan and think differently beyond Sunday morning. Here's the hard truth and great opportunity that is before us: Sunday is no longer the only day we have to create these transformative experiences that engage current members or reach our community. While Sunday is a day, it's no longer the day. While most congregations spend hours planning what happens on Sunday morning between the hours of 8:00 a.m. and 12:00 p.m., we have no clear strategy for the other 164 hours of the week . . . until now. By embracing decentralized and flexible approaches to faith formation and engaging new audiences, this book provides solutions that fit into people's everyday lives, rather than requiring them to adjust to traditional church schedules. It aims to creatively and strategically leverage the other 164 hours of the week to be the church in the world. Not. Just. Sundays.

Reading the Cultural Signs

Ministry is highly influenced by context and impacted by culture. This is not to suggest that culture drives ministry or that the church simply reflects the current climate. However, ministry does not exist in a vacuum. There was a reason why Jesus used analogies of salt, light, and seeds; they represented the cultural context of his community. The people that your church is called to serve and reach are influenced and affected by the current culture. Unless ministry takes these different cultural nuances into account, it runs the risk of being irrelevant and appearing out of touch. Fruitful ministry is strategic and intentional about adjusting to these changes. In the last four to five years, our culture has undergone dramatic shifts, directly affecting how we approach and strategize around reaching new audiences and further engaging the current congregation. These changes impact how we view ministry, revealing fresh possibilities that extend beyond Sunday. Let's take a closer look at some of the key shifts that are already reshaping how we think about ministry and will continue guiding our approach in the days ahead.

On-Demand: Times Are Obsolete

It's the church's newest formidable competitor. It has emerged with a vengeance and doesn't appear to be slowing down. One of our greatest challenges is no longer navigating theological differences across denominations or even grappling with the decline of religious culture. For decades, research has centered around the "de-churched" and the "nones and dones," identifying a growing number of people who lack strong connections to institutional church.

While these trends still exist, there is now a more pressing shift in culture that demands our attention: the battle against time. We are no longer just competing with changing belief systems or secularism; we are competing with relentless, busy schedules. Demanding work commitments and impossible family calendars have become the norm. Extracurricular activities, coupled with exhausting commutes, dominate evenings and weekends. We are vying for attention against dinnertime, social obligations, household chores, bedtime routines, vacations, hobbies, workouts, and homework. The demands on time have never been more pressing.

As both a pastor and a parent, I encounter this reality daily. My wife and I, both in ministry, juggle our roles with raising three children who are actively involved in athletics and extracurricular activities. Like many families, our afternoons and weekends are filled with carpools, practices, games, and events. Free time feels like a luxury. In conversations with other parents, I find a mix of comfort and discomfort in realizing how normal this experience is. Time is no longer just fleeting; it's fought over.

But this wasn't always the norm. There was a period when anticipation was built into our lives. Many of us grew up waiting eagerly for the weekly release of our favorite TV show. One had to wait an entire week to find out how the story continued, and writers intentionally crafted cliffhangers to keep us coming back. We planned our lives around these moments, knowing reruns were never guaranteed. The same structure extended to the church: Bible studies happened on specific evenings, small groups met at regular times, and outreach events had clear start and end points. As church leaders, we could confidently expect people to plan their lives around what we deemed to be important.

But times have shifted. We moved from enduring weekly frustrations to the freedom of recording shows and watching them at our convenience. Eventually, even that evolved. Today, we can binge entire seasons, and missing a release no longer carries the same weight. On-demand culture has revolutionized how people engage with these scheduled commitments. The shift from scheduled events to accessible engagement has fundamentally changed expectations. Set times are becoming increasingly obsolete as communities prioritize flexibility and seek opportunities with a longer life span.

For the church, this cultural shift presents unique challenges. Time constraints often prevent people from fully engaging in ministry opportunities. Busy schedules hinder meaningful participation and deeper connections. As ministry leaders, we frequently hear a familiar counterargument: If people cared enough, they'd make time for it. If people made God a priority, they'd attend church events. What if they didn't have to always choose between their regular obligations and church commitments? What if we shifted how we viewed engagement, recognizing that the on-demand culture isn't the enemy but an opportunity?

Values versus Activities

During the 2021 Super Bowl, Anheuser-Busch aired a poignant commercial that illustrated an essential element of the human experience. As the commercial seamlessly moved through a variety of scenarios of celebrations, accomplishments, apologies, inconveniences, and tragedies, there was a common invitation to "Let's grab a beer." They mentioned nothing about the taste or price of their product. As the commercial ended, we were reminded, "It's not really about the beer." It was a subtle but powerful nod to the deeper need for human connection, unity, and shared moments.

It's tempting for churches to stay focused *on the beer*: the many activities, programs, and products that we offer. But what if church really isn't about the beer at all? The critical question most churches ask when contemplating new ways to reach their community or deepen engagement is often, "What do we have to *do*?" This focus on activity can overshadow a more essential inquiry: "Who is God calling us to become?" Churches today are increasingly defined not by their activities but by their values. Who you are as a church is more important than what you do.

What has shifted in our culture is a growing emphasis on beliefs and behaviors. People are increasingly less concerned about what we do and more about who we are. Your community wants to know your guiding principles: What are your beliefs, why do you believe, and how will they feel when they interact with your congregation? These include the values that you openly profess and the ones that are unspoken.

Beneath the shift from activity-based engagement to a values-driven approach is a deeper need for people to feel psychologically safe. In a world where trust in institutions is declining, one of the most fundamental questions people are asking—whether they realize it or not—is, "Am I going to feel safe here?" Without that foundation of trust, no amount of programming will truly sustain long-term belonging.

Recalling the goals we set for new guests in 2020, there was one common theme that connected them to our congregation: our values. St. Luke's continues to strive to be an inclusive congregation, one that is willing to discuss difficult topics with courage and compassion. As people were looking for a place to belong, there was a constant affirmation of our values, not necessarily our activities or robust programming. For our new guests, who we were and what we believed mattered. Ironically, during COVID-19, when we had to suspend most of our normal activities and programming, that did not deter us from both reaching and attracting new people. Even those who continue to connect with us online from different cities and communities often do so because there isn't a local congregation that shares their same beliefs.

Your community wants to know who you are and how they will feel when they experience your community. You can have the most dynamic worship experience and offer a list of exciting programming, but in today's culture, it's not always about the beer.

How We Gather: Community

A so-called expert of the law asked Jesus a profound question that changed much about how we perform ministry today. In a failed attempt to test Jesus, he asked, "Who is my neighbor?" Jesus responds by telling the parable of the Good Samaritan. At the time, it was a radical response. However, Jesus uses the man's question to redefine how his listeners approach and interpret community. It was no longer defined by race or religion. Nor was it simply limited to geographic proximity. Jesus widens the circles and includes those who were traditionally excluded. It's a theme that we often find during Jesus's ministry. Whether it was eating with sinners, visiting the home of a known tax collector, touching the sick, or walking through Samaria to meet a woman at the well, Jesus consistently challenged their idea of neighbor and widened the possibilities of community.

In some ways, COVID-19 had the same effect. In fact, the US Surgeon General's warning about the epidemic of isolation highlights the deeper truth that people are wired for connection, and in a post-COVID-19 world, the ways people seek, find, and build connections are more important than ever. The pandemic helped us to redefine "our neighbor" and expand our community. It invited us to rethink and reimagine how people were finding connection and how we gathered. We now live in a world where connection is no longer determined by proximity. Technology has provided the means for people to maintain and find new connections without being in the same time zone. The counter argument for many is, "That's not authentic community!" Some define community as being able to be in the same room, looking at each other face-to-face. While it may not be for some, it is quite real for others. Let's examine how some are finding neighbors in new ways.

During the pandemic, the popularity of Peloton bikes skyrocketed. For those who were used to regular exercise, this gave them another alternative. What made this experience unique was not just the convenience it offered, but the community that gathered around it. People not only worked up a sweat, but they found "neighbors" on a similar journey. One could choose an isolated experience, but also virtually ride with friends and other real people. The Peloton Facebook group even allowed one to join various affinity groups to share pictures, progress, and ask general questions. Newcomers sought advice on how to simply clip the shoes onto the bike. On a national platform seen by thousands of other riders, people often posted vulnerable pictures of their fitness goals. It's amazing to see the words of encouragement and inspiration that were shared in response. One post that caught my attention was an individual who shared pictures of their first ride after their long, difficult journey with stage-four cancer. Fellow riders, most of whom they will likely never meet in person, shared the most heartfelt and thoughtful responses. It was a powerful reminder that connection looks different for everyone. It comes in all shapes, sizes, and places, and often shows up in ways we least expect.

Playlist

Growing up in the early 1980s and 1990s, my first introduction to music was my older brother's records. As I got older, songs were placed on cassette tapes with a side A and B. Trying to find the beginning of my favorite song was often a challenge and took skill to find the exact ratio of pressing play and stop on the stereo. As technology improved, CDs were introduced, and this problem was rectified by merely pressing one button. Then we shifted to a playlist. On one device, people could listen to a multitude of genres, styles, and artists. The listener was no longer confined to the limits of outdated media; they had options.

Just as a music playlist is curated from multiple artists, genres, and moods to fit individual preferences, needs, and circumstances, people increasingly build their spiritual playlists from a variety of sources. Your church is not the only option when it comes to answering the critical questions or concerns they have about life and faith. It is not the sole source of spiritual formation or community connection but instead one important "track" in a broader spiritual journey. The average person in the pew has options—social media content, nonprofit organizations, books, TED Talks, and a host of other voices and experiences that guide their everyday decisions.

Preachers, it's likely that you are not the only voice of influence for your congregation or community. They can access other preachers with a click of a button. They can visit their local bookstore and read the newest release from the latest "expert." One church, one preacher, one small group may not fit every spiritual need that might exist.

This was heightened during the pandemic. I was amazed by the idea that several people who worshipped with us on Sundays were already connected to other congregations. Several who joined small groups or Bible studies were committed to other churches. Just recently, I taught a class on leadership based on a book by John Maxwell, and members from other local congregations were in attendance. It does not mean their loyalty is cheapened. It simply suggests that people are now more willing to curate experiences from other genres and voices that speak to their current needs.

Churches are invited to consider how they can intentionally contribute to this playlist by offering authentic, meaningful, and complementary experiences, rather than competing with other options. It's a shift from the *church* being the center to the *person* being the center. The focus now becomes creating a unique sound that resonates with people while embracing the partnerships and collaborations with other entities and voices that will enrich the lives of those in the community. By embracing this mindset, churches can engage their communities more effectively by positioning themselves as a valuable part of a broader spiritual ecosystem while representing the diverse ways people connect with God and each other.

Technology

This is still one of the most controversial shifts that still exists. Even if you don't agree with it, technology has transformed the way we work, communicate, and navigate daily life. This is our new reality. A global pandemic has accelerated this transformation, embedding technology so deeply in our daily routines that we have become reliant on its presence. There is virtually no aspect of our lives that remains untouched by technology. Whether we are texting family members, logging into a Zoom call, sending an email, ordering an Uber, booking a hotel room, scheduling appointments, adjusting the thermostat, or using an app-based service, the impact is undeniable. Education depends more on virtual learning experiences, and even healthcare relies heavily on telemedicine and digital records. This digital and technological revolution has reshaped every aspect of our lives, making technology an integral part of our modern existence.

If technology has fundamentally changed the way we live, we must also acknowledge how it has reshaped our experience of being the church in the world today. The integration of technology into our spiritual practices cannot be overlooked; it has revolutionized how congregations connect, engage, and spread their message. Yet, this transformation presents a significant challenge for many church leaders who struggle to adapt. Too often, the conversation around technology is framed as an either/or scenario. Many leaders underestimate the profound impact technology has on their ability to engage members and reach new audiences. Others may utilize technology but do so without a coherent strategy.

However, we have reached a critical juncture where embracing technology is not optional but essential. Social media, artificial intelligence, and websites are major components of modern ministry approaches. The context in which we are doing ministry is highly reliant on technological tools. How we prayerfully and faithfully respond to this growing need will play a role in our effectiveness. For instance, your website is still the front door of your congregation. Long before people experience your physical presence, they will input your church's name into a search bar. What is your current online presence? Is it helping or hindering your attempts to reach new people? Have you considered the many ways your congregation is already using it in their daily lives? In my consulting work with churches, I often begin by evaluating their online presence and website. In most instances, I can accurately assess their growth and outreach potential based solely on their digital footprint.

One of the major reasons for the church's hesitancy is the perceived notion that this approach excludes older demographics. On numerous occasions, I encounter churches that absolve themselves from this conversation with limited knowledge and data around this assumption. Will everyone completely understand or master every digital ministry approach? Absolutely not. However, using technology strategically can actually help older demographics stay more connected and engaged.

As St. Luke's leaned more into its digital presence during the pandemic, I noticed another unexpected trend. Our older members were the demographic we were reaching at a higher rate. Our largest audience on Facebook comprised women over the age of 65. One of the most impactful Care Ministry projects was delivering tablets to seniors so they could continue to worship with us online. As we reviewed our Sunday morning data, we found that our traditional service had (and still does) the highest online chat engagement. I continue to encounter individuals who are unable to attend in-person gatherings due to health reasons or limited transportation, yet they still feel connected because of what they are able to experience online through small groups. As technology continues to advance, the challenge lies not only in using it effectively and appropriately but also in ensuring that it enhances rather than replaces genuine human experiences. This topic will be explored in further detail to highlight the immense possibilities technology offers.

Ground Rules

Let's set some ground rules as we journey together:

1. Learn from anywhere and anyone.

A good idea can come from anywhere in the room. I have learned to never limit what and whom God can use. There are moments found throughout the Bible when God uses people and communities to bring about God's will that were outside of traditional choices. God looked beyond backgrounds, locations, abilities, and even faith expressions. Whether it was a foreign nation, a gentile leader, an unfortunate outcome, or even an unplanned disruption, God used it all! So will we.

Throughout this book, I will use a variety of congregations as examples of the various concepts discussed. Some will be named, and others will only be described by location or specific ministry. This was done intentionally so that we would not be distracted by the congregation's size, denomination, or theology. While it's true that these factors play a role in constructing the congregation's culture, there are learning possibilities and potential to be seen beyond similar churches and even faith-based institutions. It gives one the opportunity to learn from different voices and the chance for God to speak through unfamiliar places. God is moving in congregations completely different than the one you represent, and this book gives one the opportunity to gain insight into these new spaces. I even invite us to look beyond the local church and see how other communities and industries are responding to the change in culture that is before us. This is simply a discipline of listening and watching wherever the Holy Spirit is moving.

2. Don't copy and paste.

It's as easy as hitting a few buttons. If only ministry were that simple. It's tempting to simply recreate and replicate a good idea. However, what's present in one space can't always be transferred to another. With many of the examples and ideas presented, there will exist a temptation to either repeat the same action or to discount it simply because it can't be identically replicated in your context. That's not the ultimate goal.

What works for one church may not work for you. Consider the principle that drives the action. Reflection, discernment, and thoughtfulness help to determine how certain strategies can be expressed in your context. Customize it. Tailor it. Maybe it sparks a new idea or uncovers an entirely new way of thinking about an aspect of your ministry. That does not mean that learning isn't possible. It will just require your own reflection to determine what ministry approach will be most effective given your context and capacity. If you are simply looking for easy answers or ways to push a few buttons, this book will not be helpful. But there are moments when the spirit moves in us, and we see what's possible through others.

3. Be curious.

Approach this book with a willingness to set aside preconceived notions and a readiness to explore fresh perspectives. We all have a default setting. I have one. Every leader has one. It exists in every church. It's where many churches are still operating today. We revert to these settings when the following occurs:

- We are in a crisis or periods of uncertainty

- We experience major transitions

- We feel a shortage in resources

- We lack a clear vision or direction

The longer we remain in church, something happens to our curiosity. Our wonder wanes with each passing year while we cycle through holy days and programming. We sing songs that convey messages that remind us of God's new mercies, morning by morning. And yet, when the opportunity presents itself, we retreat to the default setting. If you still believe in *the* church, this means that you still believe in *your* church. Let your belief open the windows of curiosity for God's spirit to create. I pray that you can recover the feeling that existed when you first experienced the power of community and the presence of grace. Trust that God can still breathe new life into you and your ministry in whatever state you find it today. So be curious. Be curious about learning. Be curious about what your congregation has yet to see or experience. Be curious about the people you haven't already reached. Be curious about what you don't know. Be curious about what we might see and experience beyond Sunday.

Beyond Sunday Reflections

1. Why do you still believe in the future of the church?

2. Compare the approach and intentionality that your church places on Sunday morning compared to the remaining days of the week. What themes emerge?

3. Who are your "neighbors"? Name the different ways people in your congregation are experiencing community.

4. How has your church changed since the pandemic? How has it been impacted by the cultural shifts that were named? Which shift(s) have you embraced? Which one(s) are you finding to be most challenging?

Chapter 2

Regroup and Reimagine

"So if anyone is in Christ, there is a new creation: everything old has passed away; see, everything has become new" (2 Cor 5:17 NRSV)! This biblical promise is both hopeful and yet equally challenging. The hope is knowing that we can experience this newness throughout our faith journeys. It reminds each of us of the possibilities of redemption when certain aspects of our lives or communities appear beyond repair. We cling to the idea that when Christ is present, there exist possibilities, fresh starts, and even resurrections. Sometimes that is the only hope to which people can cling.

There is often the spoken and unspoken fear that change is no longer possible in and around us. We sometimes fall prey to the idea that we are stuck in a vortex and must simply make the best out of unimaginable circumstances. And yet, through God's grace and sovereignty, there is always the potential of new life; something new can emerge. There's the hope that we, too, can become different people, different communities, and even different churches. This new life is not something we accomplish by ourselves, but it's through the faith we put in God that has promised that anything can be made new.

The challenge is that familiar things must sometimes fade, whether by choice or circumstance. If we truly believe in the promise of renewal, we must apply it not just to our individual journeys with God but also to our collective faith and communities. Imagine someone receiving a second chance at life but choosing to return to their old habits without any noticeable change or growth. Similarly, the church has been given an opportunity to redefine itself. We are witnessing its transformation in real time. The future church will look different from what we've known, and those that remain open to this change, embracing new ways of gathering, engaging, and serving, will continue to grow. Renewal isn't just personal; it's communal. Churches that embrace this truth will thrive now and in the future. As we grow and evolve, let's explore four ways to embrace this new season.

New Vision

In the movie *Apollo 13*, there comes a turning point when the astronauts are stranded in space, unable to return home. An explosion on the spacecraft forces them to abandon their mission to land on the moon. Engineers at NASA's Mission Control in Houston realize they need to create an improvised solution using only the materials onboard the spacecraft to help the stranded astronauts arrive safely back on Earth. In one scene, the flight director reminds the brilliant minds that have gathered together to solve the problem by acknowledging their predicament and proclaiming, "We have a new mission." Their original assignment had to be dramatically altered due to their current situation. While they had spent a large number of financial resources and years trying to get the ship to land on the moon, they had to abandon those hopes, accept a new reality, and place their remaining energy in a different direction. Their new assignment was getting the astronauts back to Earth safely.

What made them so willing to forgo their original plan? What made these different departments and agencies willing to listen and accept new plans and strategies? The answer is simple: Lives were at stake. This was a life-or-death situation. It was urgent! To stay tethered to a mission that was no longer viable would have been catastrophic. They gathered the different teams together, offered diverse perspectives, and looked at every possible option because the present circumstances demanded it.

Church, we have a new assignment. Our main goal cannot be focused on just getting people into a physical location. Too much has changed for us to simply pick up where we left off. To those who don't think this is possible in their current setting, I beg to differ. COVID-19 proved most of us wrong about the church's inability to change and adapt. Churches that were change-averse were open to experimentation, quick decisions, and flexibility. Those thought to be stuck in their old ways were willing to try something new.

If the matter were nonurgent, I think many churches would have feverishly resisted. But that was not the case. Many congregations were forced to try different methods and possibilities for connection. Even congregations that thought change was impossible had to make important decisions. Whether churches live-streamed, met on Zoom or just connected on phone calls, they made a pivot. Within a few days, many pastors had to learn how to preach to a screen and communicate to an empty room. Worship teams had to consider different possibilities for a Sunday morning worship experience. Churches experimented. We failed. We tried again. We learned. We failed. And we tried again. Many churches made significant adjustments to how they experienced faith and community during this period. If many of these changes to worship, strategy, technology, and preaching had been made just a few weeks prior, there would have been pandemonium! Heads would have turned, jobs would have been lost, and churches would have split. But we did so because it was urgent. A global pandemic will have that effect. We learned that change was and is possible.

What's unfortunate is that many churches have simply returned to their regularly scheduled programming. They reverted to their default settings. When the global pandemic was no longer a major focus, or when we convinced ourselves that the situation was no longer urgent, we simply returned to business as usual. However, there was a small percentage of churches that approached this strategically. They took on a different assignment. They regrouped and became open to a new vision that emerged. They saw possibilities and used it to their advantage. They kept the urgency. They saw the need for a community that was craving connection and accessible faith.

Referring to the spacecraft, the flight director in *Apollo 13* made a compelling case when he responded, "I don't care what it was designed to do, I want to know what it can do!" That's what's possible with a new vision. It can invite us to think differently about the prescribed, preset, predetermined approaches to ministry and allow God to show us again what we can do. What's possible through worship? What's possible in how we learn and experience community? What can VBS do? What can serving do? What can worship and technology do?

When we transitioned back to in-person worship services at St. Luke's, my role shifted to providing vision and oversight to our online community. The numbers necessitated this decision. We had become a different church: 40 to 50 percent of our worshipping community continued to worship online! Those numbers have stayed consistent to this day. That dramatically changed our Sunday morning experience and our weekly programming, and we had to rethink how people stayed engaged and connected.

If you haven't already done so, now is the time. It's not too late. Have you revisited the church's vision and new ways to live out the mission, considering today's needs? If this seems daunting, Lovette Weems describes vision simply as God's next faithful step. What is that one, next faithful step God might be asking you to take? If you are having difficulty considering why it's this important, consider the urgency. Consider the five names, the *Five Faces*, that you listed in chapter 1 and what's at stake. I'm encouraged to report, "Houston we don't have a problem, but an opportunity."

New Rhythms

Most churches have natural rhythms. They have set times throughout the course of the year when engagement and attendance ebbs and flows. Again, this is quite contextual and can be highly impacted by your surrounding area. These rhythms can be affected by the weather, the start of the new school year, summer activities, sports schedules, seasons for crops, and much more. As a former pastor in a popular tourist destination in southern New Jersey, I knew that as the summer approached, there would be an influx of people visiting the city. This dictated many events, concerts, and other communal activities being offered.

The church's previous engagement strategies heavily relied on this established, predictable programming. These rhythms created a structure centered around weekly expectations, encouraging attendance at worship services, small groups, Bible studies, events, and other activities. This consistency allowed for a reliable and expected rhythm within the church community. As churches planned various events, they often drew on past metrics that provided dependable insights into participation and attendance numbers.

However, our understanding of consistency and participation has evolved significantly. Today, consistency is no longer defined by the expectation of weekly involvement and attendance. Instead, it may manifest as attendance every other week, twice a month, or on the first Monday of each month. For some, consistency might be limited to the more temperate months, such as between April and November. For others, it appears sporadic and unpredictable. Lives are in constant flux, leading to changes in time commitments and family schedules. As a result, consistency now looks different for everyone and can take various forms, reflecting the diverse realities of modern life.

The church now faces a growing tension: Our ministries are often structured around commitments that no longer align with the natural rhythms of the people we aim to reach. For many, the places of connection, transformation, and involvement demand long-term commitments characterized by predictability. Our traditional ideas of engagement required weekly attendance, weekly serving, weekly giving, and weekly participation in small groups. However, this rigid expectation does not reflect the new realities of the world in which we now live. Fewer people are able to engage in every aspect of church life consistently at the same time, yet we continue to plan, teach, and prepare as if they should. This disconnect highlights the urgent need for churches to rethink their approach to engagement and their heavy reliance on predictable rhythms.

Remember that time is of the essence. So, how do we plan for the inconsistency and unpredictable nature of people's lives? What if there were a way to reframe our ideas around consistency to further engage and reach new communities? Does your programming reflect the current rhythms of the intended audience? This does not suggest that churches lower their expectations of engagement, but it is an invitation to create other opportunities that might reflect the reality of these new rhythms.

Here's how one pastor is approaching these new rhythms. Her congregation currently has two traditional services on Sunday mornings, and their leadership has decided to launch a contemporary service in hopes of reaching more young families in their community. Strategically, they have concluded that while their current services are connecting well with an older demographic, there just isn't a large market in their community for traditional forms of worship. However, they have polled, inquired, and acknowledged the busyness of the demographic they are trying to reach. At the moment, they are only planning on launching a new modern service once a month. That's it. The remaining Sundays will be an invitation to a serving opportunity, a small group, and a new podcast episode. In addition, their youth are currently meeting on Sunday nights due to their increased weekend activities, and the only goal is to slowly introduce an experience that aligns with the natural rhythms of their intended audience.

The Director of New Here Ministry at St. Luke's is focused on helping new individuals quickly connect to the congregation. While the church offers a variety of small groups and classes, they follow a seasonal rotation. She observed that newcomers had few opportunities to engage without making a multi-week commitment, particularly when their introduction to the church didn't coincide with the start of a new group or class. To address this, the church is developing ongoing Sunday morning experiences that highlight key values and offer learning opportunities connected to our church. These experiences will be available weekly, allowing newcomers to connect at any time. They can choose to attend one class or return for others in subsequent weeks, or simply engage with different offerings based on their schedule or rhythm of life.

New Church

For generations, the phrase "going to church" shaped how we understood faith, reinforcing the idea that church was primarily a place rather than an identity. While few would openly admit it, much of our focus revolved around a building and a schedule. Then, COVID-19 forced a shift. When gathering in a physical space was no longer an option, we had to wrestle with what it truly meant to *be* the church. No longer confined by an address, a single day, or even traditional activities, the church is evolving once again. The future of the church will not be defined by where we gather but by how we live out our faith in every space we inhabit. This is not a departure from the church's history but a continuation of its ongoing transformation.

The church has undergone significant evolutions throughout history, reflecting both its response to changing cultural contexts and the underlying faith principles that have remained constant. This journey can be traced through various major "turns," each marking a shift in how God's people gather, worship, and live out their faith.

In the early stages of biblical history, the church experienced what could be described as wilderness worship. The Israelites, on their journey through the desert after the Exodus, worshipped in tents, moving from place to place with the tabernacle as their center of worship. This mobile form of worship symbolized the transient nature of their experience, and the tent represented a place where God's presence could be encountered wherever they went. This early form of worship was practical and adaptable to the circumstances of the time, emphasizing God's nearness even in uncertain or wandering moments. It was a period marked by deep reliance on God's presence and provision in the wilderness.

As they entered the promised land, a defined geographic area, the structure of worship evolved into something more permanent. This was cemented when King Solomon built the first temple in Jerusalem, marking a significant shift towards a more stationary and set place of worship. The temple, with its designated areas for priests, sacrifices, and worshippers, represented both a physical and spiritual center for Israel's identity and faith. This established a rhythm of worship in a fixed location, symbolizing stability and God's dwelling among God's people. It was a time when worship was centered in one place, and access to God was structured around the temple system, with clear boundaries between holy and common spaces.

However, *being* church continued to evolve. When the Israelites were exiled to foreign lands, the question of worship and experiencing God became more complicated. How could they maintain their identity as God's people when they were removed from their sacred space? It's why the psalmist asked the question, "How could we sing the Lord's song in a foreign land" (Ps 137:4). This shift was a recognition that worship was not bound by a specific location but could take place wherever God's people gathered in God's name.

Jesus's message further transformed the concept of worship when he declared that the church was not a physical building but the body of believers. "For where two or three are gathered in my name, I'm there with them" (Matt 18:20). Jesus charged his followers with the understanding that the church existed within them, not in a specific temple or designated space. This radical shift opened the door for a decentralized form of worship, one that was no longer confined to a specific location but could occur wherever believers gathered.

The Apostle Paul further developed this idea by meeting in homes, where small groups of believers could come together to worship, pray, and study. Early Christians did not have grand buildings or temples; they met in intimate settings, reinforcing the concept that the church was not a structure but a living, breathing community of believers.

Today, the church finds itself at another major turn: It is now officially hybrid. Hybrid ministry is a dynamic approach to faith formation and community engagement that extends beyond the traditional church setting, blending in-person and digital spaces with everyday gathering places. The church now meets in person, in digital spaces, and wherever life happens. It recognizes that sacred space and connecting with God doesn't just happen in the sanctuary, but online and even in homes, workplaces, coffee shops, soccer fields, and the many communal spaces where people naturally connect. This approach to ministry reflects the biblical truth that wherever we go, God's presence goes with us—just as scripture reminds us, "Every place on which you set foot shall be yours" (Deut 11:24). This transforms everyday moments into sacred encounters. By embracing this shift, the church is reclaiming the principle that holy ground isn't about a location or even a particular day of the week. But *being* church happens wherever God's people are actively engaged in community and reflect the heart and love of God.

New Skills

This will be one of the church's biggest challenges. In my work with several congregations, this is the barrier. As I stated in chapter 1 (and will repeat several times), churches want to grow but aren't well-equipped. What's missing are the necessary skills needed to do ministry effectively in today's context. The good news is that skills can be learned and acquired. As the church continues to evolve and change, new skills are needed for a rapidly changing world.

As communities shift, technology advances, and new generations seek meaning and community in different ways, both clergy and laity must develop new skills to foster church growth and engagement. The future of your church depends on leaders who can adapt, connect across generations, embrace digital tools, build community partnerships, sustain their own mental health, and constantly stay connected to the needs of their audience. Growth will not be the result of simply trying harder at what worked previously or even currently, but courageously reimagining how the church can continue being a vibrant, relevant, transformative presence in people's lives. Now more than ever, clergy and lay members must commit to learning, innovating, and leading in new ways to ensure the church thrives not just for today, but for the years ahead.

Let's examine several of these skills needed for this new landscape. This is not an exhaustive list by any means, but one that highlights those mostly related to *content development*. The skills related to a more relational approach will be covered in chapter 3. As we consider the skills needed to reach and engage people beyond Sunday morning, this area continues to be the one where the largest learning curve exists. Its importance is high, and yet one where leaders receive the least amount of training and development. For the foreseeable future, it will continue to serve as the primary entry point for many new guests. The online space has become the largest mission field to date, with everyone the church aims to reach now present there. Social media is a consistent place of connection across generations. YouTube has over two billion monthly users and is accessible in over one hundred countries. Platforms such as Facebook, Instagram, and TikTok each paid billions of dollars to content creators this past year. And yet, digital strategies continue to be viewed with skepticism or used with little to no strategy.

Those who are hesitant to use it or oppose it altogether, approach it as evidence of a culture that is driven by consumption. While that can certainly be true, let's add a fuller perspective. Digital resources do more than just deliver content. We have reached a point in our culture where these mediums shape how people think, engage with ideas, and how their daily lives are impacted, anytime and anywhere! Content is rarely passively absorbed. These digital resources don't just inform, but they play a critical role in forming opinions, shaping behaviors, and forming connections in a world that extends far beyond the Sunday morning experience. These basic tools allow churches of any size to strategically connect and engage with audiences of any demographic beyond the walls of the sanctuary and the worship experience.

Short Clips

Short clips or videos are quick, engaging pieces of content that usually last just a few seconds to a few minutes. You'll see these everywhere on platforms such as TikTok and Instagram, where they grab attention and deliver messages fast. Depending on the social media platform, there are both guidelines and optimal times to increase viewing and engagement. In our fast-paced world, these short videos are quite effective for sharing ideas and information, whether it's for inspiration, education, or promotions.

The goal is to be concise and clear. It releases one from the pressures of thinking that an experience must be long to be impactful and engaging. Remember, our culture has a short attention span. Instead of hoping that our culture suddenly changes the length of time their attention can be held, this short content can be used quite effectively. One only needs to scroll through social media as evidence. This strategy is used for selling products, showing cooking demonstrations, restaurant reviews, political commentary, make-up tutorials, and even parenting tips. It's astounding what one can convey in 90 to 120 seconds. These can also be created by taking a shorter portion from longer content (worship services, sermons, etc.) and highlighting a particular element. They are great for recaps and for previews.

There are some churches that have used these short clips masterfully. They strategically take a segment of their service, sermon, or teaching and use that to both draw others back to that experience and introduce it to new audiences. Despite all the work and effort that we place into creating lengthy, in-person experiences, rarely will people watch or rewatch in its entirety. However, our chances of them engaging increases dramatically if placed within a shorter, more manageable clip. Remember: the shorter, the better.

Webinars and Masterclasses

Webinars are experienced as virtual classroom sessions where experts share their knowledge on particular topics, often including a chance for participants to ask questions and sometimes engage with others on a similar learning journey. Webinars have become popular in a variety of industries and settings because they make learning accessible and interactive. Some organizations are using webinars to educate staff, train volunteers, or engage with wider audiences, letting people participate from the comfort of their homes.

Remember, how people receive and share information is dramatically determined by individual needs and preferences. (We will discuss this further in chapter 3.) What questions might your community be asking? How do you talk to your children about race? How do you save for college or retirement? How do you maintain healthy relationships with close friends and family with different political views? It is highly likely that your audience is asking a host of questions like these and searching for answers; they just aren't depending on the church for guidance. What are the core struggles individuals are facing when it comes to their finances, faith, and family life? What value can your congregation add to those in your church and community as they wrestle with their own "how-tos"?

MasterClass is a streaming platform that offers exclusive lessons from world-renowned experts across a variety of fields. Its core message is simple: "Learn from the best, be your best." Subscribers gain unlimited access to thousands of bite-sized lessons, covering topics such as career and leadership development, acting, music, writing, cooking, fitness, and even interior design. Master-Class has strategically created a platform designed to add value for those seeking to improve their skills and knowledge in these areas. People want to learn and connect with people they trust.

There is a pastor in New Jersey who has extended the reach of his congregation and connected with new audiences by intentionally using webinars. He has taught webinars on various topics but centers his teachings around reading and interpreting the Bible for everyday living. There is another pastor in the Cleveland area who has strategically used leadership webinars to invite others far beyond her local community to engage in the journey of increasing their influence and skills during these challenging times. Both used their own influence and voice to answer critical needs or skills others desired to learn. Do people feel safe and confident turning to your congregation with their deepest questions and concerns?

Articles and Blogs

Writing still works. People read, and they read often. The effective use of digital platforms allows writing content such as articles and blogs to be easily distributed to the reader through several avenues. While both are valid content, they serve quite different purposes. Articles are normally longer, more formal, researched based, and appear in more traditional media outlets. Blogs are often shorter and informal. Sometimes, they can be conversational; often designed for engagement, sharing, and eliciting immediate responses from readers. The reader will either connect with this content through intentional and topic-related searches or by subscription. The material can be easily accessible, appearing directly on the reader's device. Some have used this content for educational purposes, responding to an important event, or simply documenting a first-hand experience. Like many others, this form of content can live on well beyond its release date. Your community can revisit and engage this content as they see fit for an extended period of time. Consider the number of times you have searched for information and noticed that the article was months, and sometimes even years, old. There are many topics that are timeless in the human experience, as well as those that require constant revision and adaptation. Writing gives authors the opportunity to directly share these ideas with readers, and, when used strategically, it can have a powerful impact.

Of the many tools available, this is one of the most underutilized yet cost-effective strategies available for churches. Consider the critical and urgent information that's needed for your audience and the impact of receiving relevant information from a voice they know and trust. Every day, I receive content sent directly to my email about various subjects, ranging from church growth to relationships to health-related topics. I've used the content to make decisions about my own approach to ministry, how I plan date nights, and what meals I plan for the week. The information mattered. I read it. I use it. And I continue to refer to it. Why? Because it adds value.

There is another church in the Midwest that has an entire page on its website devoted to written content. The content is grouped into the following categories: culture, money, relationships, self, and work. Some of the titles include, "Dear Manager, I'm Going on Maternity Leave," "Valentines Day Gift Ideas When You're Not Feeling It," "My Back to School Was a Hot Mess, How Was Yours?," "Feeling Pressure to Get Your Child a Phone? Try This," or "Quit Asking Why I'm Single." All articles have accompanying estimated reading times, many of which are no more than eight to eleven minutes. However, it's clear that the church has identified accessible strategies of adding value to their audience through simple articles and blogs.

Interviews

Interviews, which involve conversations between two or more individuals, are a powerful medium for sharing stories and insights. This form of engagement has gained significant traction in media, research, and content creation, as society increasingly values authentic voices and personal experiences. This trend reflects our growing appetite for varied perspectives—from everyday individuals to celebrated figures such as former athletes and public personalities. Interviews create accessible conversations that often resonate more deeply than traditional lectures or sermons, breaking down barriers and fostering genuine connection.

At St. Luke's, we have harnessed the power of interviews over the past few years, effectively integrating them into our church culture. The Senior Pastor has often used interviews as a part of the Sunday morning worship experience, interviewing past guests such as former Olympians, professional basketball coaches, a current and former governor of Indiana, and local television personalities. During the pandemic, he further extended this content through our preservice learning opportunity, "Anchor Point," inviting influential figures like Jim Wallis, writer and founder of

Sojourners, a magazine, and Bryan Stevenson, a lawyer and the founder of Equal Justice Initiative, to share their insights. We have interviewed members, community leaders, and others impacted by our ministries.

Mastering the art of conducting meaningful interviews can yield impactful benefits. First, it exposes congregants to fresh ideas and diverse perspectives, offering access to voices they might otherwise never encounter. Hearing different viewpoints broadens the congregation's understanding of God's activity in the world and highlights often-overlooked narratives. Secondly, this approach fosters strategic partnerships, creating opportunities for future relationships within the community. Additionally, interview content is incredibly versatile—it can be repackaged, reformatted, and repurposed into short clips, enabling the message to be revisited often. A single interview can serve multiple formats, maximizing its reach. Consider the overlooked voices and experiences that your congregation needs to encounter. What vital perspectives from the community should they be hearing during this critical time? By embracing interviews as an essential aspect of your church's content strategy, you can cultivate a richer, more inclusive faith experience.

Repurposed Content

Repurposed content means taking existing material and transforming it into new formats, such as turning a webinar into a blog post or converting a short video into an infographic. It can even include using portions of the same content on the same platform, just at a different time during the year. For example, using content created around finances doesn't just have to be shared during your stewardship months. People need to hear about generosity more than once a year. Or a short clip can be taken from an impactful interview that may correspond with something related to a recent event in your community or national conversation.

Consider the practical use of repurposed content. Most pastors spend hours crafting their sermons on a weekly basis. For many, once the sermon (or any content) is over, it is rarely revisited. In fact, there is often a disdain and hesitancy around reusing the same content or ideas. One pours one's heart into developing a message, only to place it on a shelf, rarely to be used again. Our culture has shifted the expectation and use of content. Think of the number of movies and television shows you have watched repeatedly. Most of the reels and videos people view online and on social media platforms are often weeks and sometimes even years old! Often, you are not even viewing content from the original owner, but what someone else has decided to share. There are certain timeless themes and messages that have the potential to impact your audience well beyond their release or posted date.

This highlights two experiences from which the church can learn. First, audiences are less concerned about when it was created and more interested in whether it connects with their lives and current experiences. There are certain themes, questions, and words of inspiration that we need to be reminded of constantly and consistently. We spend hours crafting material to reach a particular subset of our community, and we limit its potential by quickly moving on and never revisiting the experience. Lean into revisiting what people desperately need to hear. Revisit those values that will shape your church and community.

Remember, what's old to you has the potential to be new to someone else. If you are truly reaching new people, they will be experiencing and hearing much of what you share with new eyes. We would like to believe that people remember everything we've ever written or preached, but they don't. Don't hesitate to intentionally and strategically reuse and repurpose the messages and experiences that continue to connect with your congregation.

While there are countless examples of its use, one church located near the Washington, D.C. area, found a way to creatively use previous content for New Year's Eve. As a way of celebrating with their congregation and wider community, they replayed the pastor's favorite sermons from the year throughout the day, inviting people to revisit them as they anticipated the year ahead. It drew interest from both current and new audiences.

Live-Streaming

Live events are real-time experiences or discussions where people engage directly with each other or speakers. With live-streaming platforms and social media continuing to increase, these events have become an easy, affordable vehicle for churches to connect instantly with their audience. They create a sense of community and engagement, making for a more immersive experience compared to prerecorded content.

I was facilitating a cohort with Presbyterian pastors from Michigan, Ohio, and Indiana. Their major concern was the cost that's often associated with connecting with audiences digitally. However, one pastor of a small, rural congregation shared that they strategically invite their Sunday morning worshipping community to join a "live" Wednesday night conversation around the topics of the previous sermon. It provided a way for the pastor to not only go deeper into the sermon but also gave others an opportunity to ask questions and engage in a different manner.

There is another United Methodist pastor from a very large congregation who hosts live vespers services weekly, which includes conversations and thoughtful discussions. It not only provides a similar level of community expressed by the Presbyterian pastor, but also invites a certain level of accessibility that's not always present in larger congregations. This is a congregation that has several campuses and several services on Sunday mornings. And yet, this live encounter provides an informal opportunity to connect with their spiritual leader regardless of their worshipping campus.

Podcasts

Podcasts are programs you can listen to or watch at any time and from anywhere, and they cover a variety of topics. They continue to rise in popularity because they offer flexibility and allow us to connect with content and the creators while on the move. Over one hundred million people regularly listen to podcasts! It is a growing platform that continues to expand and easily connects with those demographics that the church does not easily reach. Notice the strategic use of this medium of your favorite athletes, authors, or even comedians. Many use podcasts to share insights and tell stories, creating connections in a format that fits busy lifestyles effectively.

This has become one of the most popular ways that people give and receive information. Some take on a variety of formats, from solo presentations to inviting different guests with differing perspectives. While there can be an initial cost of set up and time for prep and recording, it has the potential of high reach, while being quite affordable. My wife wakes up every morning and listens to NPR podcasts. I often listen to podcasts on the long drives escorting my kids to their out-of-town soccer tournaments. Depending on the demographics of your community, there are certain voices that hold an immense amount of authority. They tune in with regularity. They sign up for new episodes. And they listen or watch at their leisure. There are some churches that host a weekly podcast with the pastoral staff to discuss the sermon or topics within their community.

One church in the Midwest has done a masterful job using podcasts to not only connect with their community, but also to engage in larger conversations. They have leaned into this medium, offering a variety of different podcasts that reach diverse segments of their community. The different podcast categories revolve around topics such as surviving grief, asking and answering random questions people may ask, money and finances, parenting, local issues impacting their community, and even real stories from everyday people with close spiritual encounters. Their options are diverse, but one glance reveals their intentional approach of adding value based on the knowledge of their community in a manner that is accessible and aligns with their natural rhythms.

True renewal calls us to be bold enough to let go of what's familiar, trusting that God's guidance will lead us to something better. As we move forward, we must be ready to embrace a new vision, develop new practices, and equip ourselves with the skills needed to navigate this transformation, knowing that God's grace will always bring about growth and possibility.

Beyond Sunday Reflections

1. What new vision or assignments do you feel emerging?

2. Identify the necessary skills needed for this next faithful step. (Feel free to discuss others that are not listed. Consider your unique context and direction.)

3. Define consistency. Articulate the new life rhythms that have emerged within your congregation and community.

4. How do you differentiate between *going to* church and *being* church.

Chapter 3

Formation Happens Everywhere

It was a question that would have a lasting effect and change the way many of us approached ministry. During one of my Doctor of Ministry classes at Wesley Theological Seminary, the professor asked a thought-provoking question to the group of clergy and religious professionals: "Where have you experienced your most transformative encounters with God?" He gave us time to reflect before inviting us to share our answers. The responses were diverse. Some spoke of their peaceful, serene experiences with God in nature, such as simple walks, camping, or hiking. Others shared about encounters during creative moments like painting, songwriting, or sculpting. Some found God in places like retreat centers, gyms, and even skydiving. A few mentioned specific life events that marked their spiritual transformation, while others reflected on more ordinary settings like coffee shops or morning walks to watch the sunrise. Then, our professor posed a challenge that completely shifted the conversation.

He thanked us for our willingness to share and challenged us to consider how our vocational pursuits aligned with our spiritual experiences. He asked why a group of ministry professionals, who had encountered God in such diverse and profound ways, would spend the majority of their careers trying to get people to experience God in just one place, for one day, and within a limited time frame. He urged us to imagine a ministry that invites people to experience God in the various places where we encounter God and, even better, in the places that resonate with them. What if we shifted our focus from creating experiences centered around a physical building to helping people encounter God in the world where everyday life unfolds? What if we dedicated as much energy and attention to helping people experience God in their daily routines as we do to Sunday mornings?

I could call this an anomaly, but I've tested this theory in various settings. I've asked this same question while facilitating workshops, teaching classes, and coaching church leadership teams. And much like my own experiences, the answers vary, but one thing remains consistent: Sunday morning is never the dominant answer to how people are experiencing transformative encounters with God. Never. People are indeed encountering God everywhere!

This serves as a reminder that everyday transformative experiences play a vital role in shaping and forming faith. These informal moments highlight how faith is cultivated through ordinary, day-to-day experiences, not just on Sundays. Let me be clear, this is not about devaluing the Sunday morning worship experience. Continue to plan, execute, and give your best effort to your services. Preach with passion and preparation. But remember, Sunday is not the only place where God is present or where people are growing in their faith. Transformation is happening everywhere, and faith is being formed every day.

Similar to how we plan and prepare for Sunday mornings, we don't have to leave these everyday encounters to chance. If our mission is to make disciples and create environments where faith is constantly being nurtured, we must consider how we can plan, create, and even strategize around these experiences. At the heart of this approach is the belief that faith can be developed anywhere and transformation can occur everywhere.

This approach to faith formation will define the future church. The markers of health, vitality, and success will no longer be confined to Sunday mornings but will shift toward engagement. Relying solely on measuring Sunday morning attendance is insufficient. As digital ministry continues to grow and cultural shifts impact the church, defining faith communities based on one day of the week ignores the larger conversation about engagement that extends beyond the church walls.

Growth will be driven by a church's ability to foster engagement and create meaningful spaces for connection and formation. Viewing church attendance as merely a place to go, rather than a dynamic community of believers called to live out the ministry of Jesus in the world, limits its potential. People are not just looking for another place to go; they are seeking a community to belong to and a faith they can integrate into their everyday lives.

Beyond the Temple:
Jesus's Model for Discipleship

Let's reflect on the process Jesus used to form his disciples. Ironically, it didn't begin in the temple, on the Sabbath, or during a religious festival. The call to discipleship was initiated in the most ordinary of places: the lakes of Galilee, far from the religious center of Jerusalem. There was nothing remarkable about that day. These men were going about their daily routines, doing the same work they had done countless times. But something was different that day. The familiarity of the place, the repetitive nature of their task, and the company of the same people suddenly changed the course of their lives. Jesus met them where they were, in the midst of their everyday lives, and saw something in them that they had never seen in themselves. He offered them the chance to become something more, something greater than their current experience. He painted a vision of who they could become, a life shaped and transformed by him. In response, they left everything behind and followed him. The call was not simply to attend a religious gathering, but to live a life of discipleship, following Christ in every aspect of their being.

Jesus kept his promise. Over the course of three years, he shaped them into people who would learn to "fish for people." But how did he form their faith? How did he disciple them? These were fishermen, tax collectors, and people from various walks of life. And yet, Jesus used the ordinary, everyday experiences of life to shape and form them into his disciples. Their faith formation didn't happen in the confines of a temple or a scheduled religious service. Instead, it occurred in the midst of real life. A simple wedding became the place where Jesus demonstrated his power, turning water into wine. The disciples heard the core teachings of Jesus—like the Sermon on the Mount—spoken from a place many had previously visited, yet it became a pivotal moment in their understanding of his kingdom. They witnessed his power firsthand when he calmed a storm during a routine boat ride across the lake, or when he walked on water, showing that even the elements obeyed his voice.

The disciples' faith was also formed during hardship. After one of his most challenging moments in ministry, Jesus retreated to pray. Yet, when a crowd followed him, despite his exhaustion, he didn't turn them away. Instead, he had compassion on them, healed the sick, and fed more than five thousand with just a few loaves and fish. They saw his power and grace not only in the temple or during religious observances but also in everyday moments—in homes, on the side of the road, and in crowded spaces. Whether it was a woman touching his robe or the casting out of demons, every experience became a lesson in faith, a moment for discipleship.

The common thread in their faith formation was that it transcended the temple and set times of worship. Their everyday lives, whether in the marketplace, on a boat, at a wedding, or simply walking down the street, became the primary context for learning, growth, and transformation. Jesus didn't reserve his teaching for special occasions; he used the rhythms of daily life to shape his disciples. These experiences, ordinary and extraordinary, became the foundation of their faith, preparing them for their future ministry. Through these encounters, Jesus transformed them from fishermen into fishers of people. His way of discipleship teaches us that faith formation happens not just in the church, but in the everyday moments of life, wherever we are and whatever we are doing.

Outcomes versus Activities

When reflecting on Jesus's process of discipleship and faith formation, we see an approach that differs from the traditional model many churches use today. Much of the conversation around discipleship has revolved around a prescribed set of activities. These might include actions such as worship, giving, serving, small groups, or community involvement. In the early 2000s, this activity-based approach became popular as research suggested that clarity and simplicity were more important than random, disconnected activities. Churches began to develop clear pathways, making the process of discipleship easier to follow. To support this, churches would often customize their language, branding these pathways to make them more engaging. Successful churches consistently reminded their congregants about these opportunities, reinforcing the importance of their engagement.

This clarity not only helped churches communicate their processes more effectively but also provided measurable outcomes. Attendance at Bible studies, small groups, volunteer hours, event registrations, and giving numbers became the metrics for faith formation. The underlying assumption was that the more someone engaged in activities, the more they would grow in their faith. This is a clear activity-based approach.

While these activities certainly have merit, there is often a gap between performing activities and genuinely transforming behavior. It's possible to go through the motions without ever allowing the experience to change one's heart or actions. Jesus addressed this when he rebuked the Pharisees for their emphasis on ritual over sincerity, quoting Isaiah: "This people honors me with their lips, but their hearts are far from me; in vain do they worship me, teaching human precepts as doctrines" (Matt 15:8-9). This gap between activity and transformation is evident throughout history. There have been many periods of high church activity, but often the actions didn't align with the values and ministry approach of Jesus. I've witnessed countless instances where communities were highly engaged, yet their actions did not reflect the values of Christ.

This is not to devalue the activities that foster regular engagement with faith; they are essential to spiritual growth. Brand your process. Maintain clarity. However, what if discipleship moved beyond a checklist of activities and focused instead on the outcomes or the transformation of individuals based on values defined by the congregation? An outcome-based approach shifts the focus from simply completing church activities to reflecting tangible behaviors such as love, justice, service, patience, joy, and generosity. In this model, discipleship becomes less about what I do and more about who I am becoming.

This shift is challenging because we are conditioned to ask questions like, "How many people attended?" or "How many signed up?" But what if we asked, "*What kind of disciples are we producing?*" This is one of the most important questions we can ask of our ministries. I know it's difficult to measure this using traditional methods, as most church management systems are designed to track attendance and registration, not behavior. However, the answers to this question might reveal more than the numbers ever could.

By focusing on behaviors, we can evaluate whether our activities are producing real fruit. For example, we might ask: Are we developing disciples who are comfortable sharing their faith? Are we producing disciples who prioritize their community over individual preferences? Are we fostering a generous faith community that serves with their resources and gifts? Do they have a heart for justice and inclusion?

This shift ensures that discipleship is not just a to-do list, but a transformational journey that aligns with the mission and core values of the congregation. It doesn't replace clarity or defined pathways, but it expands the opportunities for transformation beyond typical experiences. When discipleship is about the behaviors being formed, our strategy and activities should be evaluated through this lens, not just by attendance. So, don't just measure the numbers, observe the behaviors.

Engagement Is a Numbers Game

Faith formation is a numbers game, but not in the traditional sense. To truly cultivate an environment where people grow closer to God and each other, it takes time, intentionality, and a shift in how we think about engagement. Historically, discipleship revolved around clear, structured pathways with designated on-ramps for involvement. However, in a culture where time is scarce and people's schedules are full, we need to rethink our approach.

Consider this: In a given week, there are 168 hours. Let's assume, in the best-case scenario, that an individual commits to a one-hour worship service every week (rounded up to two hours to account for different faith expressions), volunteers for an hour as an usher, serves in the community for another hour, and participates in a Bible study or small group for another hour. That's approximately five hours of spiritual engagement in a given week. Out of 168 hours, that's only 3 percent of a person's time. This is the best-case scenario—assuming they are fully committed and able to dedicate time every single week. In reality, most people simply can't commit to that level of engagement. Life happens, and even those who desire to grow spiritually will likely fall short of these expectations.

Now, imagine asking people to become spiritually mature with only 3 percent of their week dedicated to discipleship and obtaining those identified values. In no other area of life would we expect such a small investment to yield such significant results. This is the core challenge: The traditional model of discipleship relies too heavily on people attending structured, church-based events, but that's no longer a sustainable path to high-level engagement. Most people don't attend worship weekly, and even fewer attend Bible studies or small groups on a regular basis. Remember, people have complex lives, changing rhythms, and limited time.

So, how do we break this cycle and truly increase engagement? The answer must look beyond adding other items to the to-do list. The answer lies in creatively integrating discipleship into people's everyday lives. Rather than trying to force more activities or events onto already busy schedules, the church must shift its focus to meeting people where they are. This doesn't necessarily mean abandoning Sunday gatherings or traditional programs, but it does mean recognizing that faith formation doesn't only happen within the walls of the church. We must strategically plan to use people's daily lives as fertile ground for spiritual growth and formation. By seamlessly weaving discipleship into the everyday experiences people already have, we can help them grow in faith without adding another item to their to-do lists. This is how we win the numbers game, not by competing for more of people's time, but by transforming the time they already have into opportunities for connection and spiritual formation.

Redefining *Hybrid?*

As we have previously stated, hybrid ministry is the new ministry. Churches that are experiencing significant growth and increasing engagement have fully embraced this approach. It is how people live their lives, and even how they encounter faith and connection. The church is not exempt to the hybrid realities of our culture. And yet, there are still many churches that have and will resist this approach.

Normally, the hesitancy is rooted in their distrust and skepticism of digital tools and platforms. Here are basic common myths that are often associated with online ministry:

- Digital investments cost too much. Finances will be a major barrier.

- Online connection is inauthentic. Serving online isn't doing "real" ministry.

- Posting and streaming are strategies.

- The end result should be an in-person gathering.

Here's the truth:

- Many affordable tools exist for digital ministry, allowing churches to start small and scale up over time, making it accessible for ANY size budget.

- Online ministry is not only authentic, but when used strategically, it can be used to enhance in-person ministry and connections.

- Use of online ministry or digital tools should be included within the larger mission and overall strategy to be most effective.

- Online ministry should still focus on discipleship and growing in faith, not just funneling people into in-person experiences.

One of the major benefits of hybrid ministry is that it helps to bridge the gap between in-person and online participants by intentionally fostering connection with those who engage digitally. Instead of being "out of sight, out of mind," online participants are valued and included in the church's community through digital touchpoints like virtual small groups, social media engagement, and online events. This approach encourages churches to think more inclusively and creatively, ensuring that every member, whether attending in person or online, has meaningful opportunities for connection, growth, and belonging.

Today, any church that relies solely on in-person experiences to provide meaningful places of connection and growth will limit its reach and impact. Many people interact with the church online as much as they do in person. As we have mentioned in previous chapters, online tools and technology can be quite effective in the faith formation beyond Sunday morning. The aforementioned tools discussed in chapter 1 can be used to strategically keep people connected to the church throughout the week, when the rhythms of life constantly change.

Some people fear the cost and skills required for using digital strategies but, remember, these tools can include everything from social media to emails to text messages. For example, BeADisciple recently launched an app designed to make small group participation more accessible. Participants can join from nearly any device, with study materials readily available within the app itself. It offers training, resources, reflections, and readings, all in one place. This platform allows people to stay connected to their congregation or faith community from anywhere in the world as they grow in faith together.

Other churches are using Bible-related apps for daily devotions or scripture reading plans; some use apps such as *Ritual: Well-Being Practices*. This app helps users create meaningful and purposeful rhythms throughout the day. Offering daily practices and spiritual disciplines such as meditation and guided reflections, it fosters intentional living and clarity that can easily be integrated into everyday life.

Perhaps it's helpful to begin with a different starting point. Instead of limiting digital ministry to helping others stay connected to the church, this approach allows the church to stay connected to its congregation. I've found it extremely helpful from a congregational care perspective. I have discovered critical information, moments of celebration, and seasons of struggle from reading the posts and status updates from those connected to the church. Unless your congregation has a perfect system where members readily share this kind of information, this may not be useful, but social media is often a place of vulnerability for many people. Over the past few years, I have had more pastoral conversations and calls based on what I've learned from others simply by online connections. I've learned about cancer diagnoses, break-ups, deaths, engagements, college acceptances, political frustrations, marriage anniversaries, birthdays, job losses and promotions, and even changes in careers. Increasing engagement is a two-way street. It allows people to increase their engagement with the church, and it also allows the church to stay connected to the many people that are connected to it.

Given this reality, hybrid ministry helps close the back door by creating multiple pathways for people to stay engaged, even when life becomes unpredictable. Whether someone is traveling for vacation, navigating health challenges, changing a work schedule, or simply adjusting to a new rhythm of life, hybrid ministry offers consistent touch points that keep them connected to the church community. Through digital content, virtual check-ins, and flexible opportunities to serve or learn, the church remains present in their lives beyond Sunday morning. This kind of connection reinforces belonging, making it less likely for individuals to quietly drift away.

One pastor of a medium-sized congregation uses intentional language in his benediction to invite his congregation to increased engagement using a hybrid approach just about every Sunday. As he is delivering parting words to those who are gathered in person and online, he invites those worshipping online to one day visit in person when the opportunity presents itself. But then, he also invites those in person to stay connected through various online opportunities throughout the week. In one simple statement and invitation, this church is casting a vision for engagement that includes every participant and acknowledges the reality of the differing ways the entire church can stay connected.

While this approach to ministry can include online and digital components, it includes so much more. It's more than just recognizing that people worship in person and online. A hybrid approach to ministry is a flexible approach to experiencing faith and community that blends a variety of in-person, digital, and self-directed experiences to meet people where they are already gathering. It is dedicated to creating meaningful experiences for people both within and beyond the walls of the church.

During COVID-19, *1000 Hours Outside* wanted to convey the value of spending time outdoors. While millions around the world were confined to their homes, they seized the opportunity to create an experience that invited people into a broader, more connected community. Through targeted digital marketing and tools, they invited people to participate in spending one thousand hours outside! There were resources available to log hours. A curriculum was created to complement the physical experience. They developed social media communities for people to connect and share their stories. It was a simple way to get people safely outside, away from their devices, and focus on something other than being quarantined in a home. It was not limited by time, space, or even location. Simply by walking outside, one could participate and engage. The outdoors became a place of experiential learning. This is a hybrid approach.

Imagine how this could be used in the context of church ministry. What if, during the warm or colder months of the year, a church was strategic about inviting those in the congregation and community to experience a similar practice by using the outdoors as a way to learn about and experience God? The Bible is filled with images and imagery of seeds, water, clouds, trees, grass, wind, rain, leaves, branches, fruit, and much more. Depending on your geographic location, the experience could be formatted to include the different seasons, using the unique opportunities to include everyday experiences. Imagine a youth or children's ministry devising a curriculum or family discussion around the color changes of the leaves or the unique design of every snowflake. The possibilities are endless. It could be a strategic invitation to find God in their everyday lives and not be confined to Sundays. This is everyday faith. You don't have to compete with vacations, sports, the beach, or overnight camps. With a hybrid ministry approach, you can literally meet them where they are.

Learning-on-the-Go

Learning is a core aspect of discipleship and faith formation because growth requires both knowledge and lived experience. Just as Jesus taught through parables, questions, and everyday interactions, learning is not just about acquiring information. It's about transformation. True learning leads to thoughtful convictions, changed behaviors, and a faith that influences daily decisions. It is an ongoing journey of learning more about God, understanding community, discovering oneself, and learning how to live better with others. Jesus's reminder to love the Lord God with all one's heart, mind, soul, and spirit reflects a holistic approach to learning. John Wesley, the founder of Methodism, emphasized the importance of immersing oneself in scripture for discipleship, believing it was essential in shaping one's heart and mind toward holiness.

While the commitment to growth and learning has remained constant, the ways in which people learn, acquire information, and are formed have undergone a major shift. We are currently experiencing another "learning revolution." This revolution marks a significant departure from traditional, one-size-fits-all learning methods. Instead, diverse, adaptive, and flexible approaches are now embraced to share and receive knowledge. People now *learn-on-the-go*. Learning-on-the-go is a process of integrating new ideas, skills, or perspectives seamlessly into daily routines, leveraging real-world experiences, conversations, and digital tools to support continuous growth. This approach assumes that learning isn't confined to specific times or places.

We see this trend across various industries and professions. It has revolutionized professional development and the acquisition of new skills, driving an increased demand for professional certifications and development. In fact, many job applications now require candidates to list additional certifications alongside their work history. This shift is driven by the flexibility of learning programs that can often be completed at the participant's convenience. While some require live teaching, most offer flexible, pre-recorded content and community connections that allow participants to learn from others in the field.

LinkedIn, an online platform for professionals, has introduced LinkedIn Learning to help users enhance their own professional development. Members can access an array of classes, resources, and training modules to support their growth, all at their own pace. These classes range in duration, from brief sessions to ones more extensive, allowing employees to engage in professional development without sacrificing their other responsibilities. This flexibility ensures that learning doesn't need to exist as a choice between career growth and competing demands.

Major universities are also embracing online learning, offering both continuing education and general education courses online. As enrollment in full-time seminary programs declines, many institutions have turned to virtual learning to reach students nationwide and globally. This learning revolution has had a profound impact across various industries and experiences.

Learning-on-the-Go and Its Role in Ministry

Ministry doesn't happen in a vacuum. Ignoring this cultural shift would not only be shortsighted but could also hinder meaningful participation in the life of the church. For most churches, embracing this new approach to learning would be radically different. For at least the last two decades, the phrase "people learn better in circles than in rows" has been the dominant narrative. This reflects a shift in how information was shared. No longer was the authority figure the sole presenter before a passive audience. Instead, circles encouraged equal sharing, inviting participants to contribute their ideas and interpretations. This shift has encouraged more collaborative learning, with lay people stepping into leadership and facilitation roles. Curriculum design has evolved to support this collaborative approach, leading to an increase in Christian education materials that foster discussion and serve as resources for group leaders.

Learning-on-the-go doesn't negate the traditional ways information is shared within the church. Certain cultural expressions of faith still rely on the pastor as the authoritative figure, and there is value in small groups where people can share their lives as they grow in faith. However, if the goal is to increase engagement, the church should be strategic in using various tools to allow members to dive more deeply into topics and perspectives, and to engage flexibly outside of preset time. Approach learning and engagement from the perspective of the learner. When are they most available? What learning environments seem to resonate with the various groups and demographics represented in your context? Are you trying to get more people into present opportunities, or are there additional ways and opportunities people can increase their learning and engagement?

We have arrived at a point in our culture when the church is no longer limited to specific times or days for helping others acquire knowledge and understanding. As a church, how can you make learning and engagement more accessible to your members?

This is more than just the consumption of information. While it doesn't replace opportunities for connection, it does invite new possibilities for increased engagement and formation. Many people in your congregation are already being shaped by the tools mentioned earlier; it's just that the church hasn't been strategic in adding its own voice to this ongoing learning revolution.

DIY (Do-It-Yourself)

The accessibility of discipleship, then, is viewed as a decentralized process inviting individuals to grow at their own pace in a do-it-yourself (DIY) model. Just as people engage in countless DIY projects, ranging from home improvement to crafting, often turning to online resources for guidance, discipleship can similarly leverage technology and its community to empower learners. Think about how many times we've needed an answer and turned to YouTube for a solution. I was at the home of a colleague, who is exceptionally talented in décor, for an intimate church gathering. On several occasions, when guests asked her how she learned to build or design something, her common response was, "I learned by watching YouTube."

In this model, individuals take ownership of their spiritual growth, utilizing various resources to explore their faith on their terms. This learner-centered approach allows for deeper engagement, as participants can choose topics that resonate with them, explore questions that arise in their personal lives, and integrate their learning into everyday experiences. By placing the learner at the center, decentralized discipleship acknowledges that faith development is not a one-size-fits-all journey. Instead, it recognizes the unique paths each person takes as they navigate their relationship with God and their community, fostering a more vibrant and diverse expression of faith.

This does not suggest that faith formation is a free-for-all with the learner being left in a world of options and possibilities to fend for themselves. Quite the contrary. It allows the church to plan and strategize differently. It encourages the church to provide clear options, helping the learner navigate a world full of voices, opinions, and theological perspectives. The church can serve as a valuable resource, pointing people to other credible voices and exposing its community to a variety of experiences.

This approach has a profound impact on family ministry. It shifts the ministry focus from simply bringing children and youth *to* church to participate in church activities to equipping parents and caregivers as active and engaged partners in their children's growth and spiritual development. Instead of relying solely on structured lessons and weekly participation at a set time, this model encourages families to create learning opportunities from everyday experiences. This can happen through conversations at the dinner table or even car rides home from school. It acknowledges that faith development for families doesn't just happen at church on a Sunday morning, but in the rhythm of daily life, where parents or caregivers play an important role in modeling and reinforcing certain values. Churches can reposition themselves as collaborators and support families with resources, ideas, discussion questions, and even creative learning experiences in ways that are more personal to the individual child. Remember that it's a numbers game. I'm reminded of one church that created a bedtime podcast, featuring various scriptures read by voices from their youth ministry. At the end of each biblical story, they invited the child or adult to pray. It was a creative way to engage both the child and the adult, incorporating the church into the everyday rhythms of the often-difficult nighttime routines.

At a previous church of one of my current colleagues, the leadership realized that many of their students were highly involved in sports. If you have students in your ministry, then you are aware of the impact that this can have on their Sunday morning attendance. Instead of seeing these extra-circulars as competition, their ministry leaders leaned into the experience and decided to use it as a means of formation and engagement. During a Sunday morning worship service, they commissioned these students to be the hands and feet of Jesus on their respective teams and sports fields. They invited those sitting in the vicinity of these students and families to place their hands on them while they prayed and blessed them for their upcoming seasons. To help reinforce this experience beyond Sunday morning, the student athletes were given devotionals to be used on the fields, along with worship playlists and Starbucks gift cards! It released the guilt that's often associated with extracurriculars, and those families felt supported. A system for engagement was created to encourage them to stay engaged-on-the-go.

Another church took this same approach and strategically used something in popular culture and paired it with Advent to increase engagement with their families. They created an immersive experience with Elf on the Shelf. For those that aren't familiar, Elf on the Shelf is a fun way to celebrate the holiday season as adults place a small elf in different places throughout the home, attached with humorous or thoughtful messages.

I must admit, we jumped on the bandwagon. Every night, we found a new place for the elf, and because we are both preachers, we tried to offer our children thoughtful messages about themselves and the coming of Christ as they started their day. There were a few nights I woke up in a panic because I forgot to move the elf! While scrolling through social media for ideas, I came across a church inviting participants to download their creative ideas for elf placements, along with supporting scriptures. Genius! All you had to do was submit your email address and receive instructions for making the experience fun and easy. It was simple, thoughtful, relevant, and it worked. The morning ritual of finding the elf became part of those families' consistent faith formation. They didn't create anything new or ask families to carve out additional time during the busy season. Instead, they invited themselves into what families were already doing and gathering around.

"Backyard VBS" is a growing, decentralized model that brings faith formation into local neighborhoods, creating meaningful connections where people live, all while remaining tied to the wider church body. Families are encouraged to invite neighbors into these intimate, familiar settings, supported by the church through curriculum, encouragement, and shared opening and closing celebrations. Last year's "Camp Firelight" theme, provided by Cokesbury, served as a perfect backdrop for this approach, transforming backyards into sacred spaces for storytelling, wonder, and transformation. It's a reminder that sacred moments can unfold around picnic tables, under trees, and within the presence of a familiar community. This is a creative expression of hybrid ministry, meeting people where they are and helping them encounter God in the places they already call home.

So, where are people already gathering? Where are they spending most of their time? Is it at home? Is it on their commute? On any given week, I spend at least five to ten hours commuting and waiting for my children to finish an extracurricular activity. I'm already in my car. You already have my attention. What would I need to hear? What could you offer me as a busy spouse and parent that I would need to hear or experience from a church? Meet me where I am already gathering. The context will vary, but the need is there. Remember that this is a numbers game. You are competing with the business of their lives and the constant demands that families have on their lives. Transform everyday experiences into places of engagement and formation. In addition to asking "How can we get families more involved?", maybe we could include, "How can the church be more involved and engaged with families?"

It's this kind of ministry that invites us into a new level of creativity, curiosity, and responsibility. It moves us beyond simply managing programs and church activities, and toward crafting moments that stay with people for a lifetime. These formative experiences anchor someone's faith journey for years to come. Think of discipleship and faith formation as a blank canvas, giving us permission to dream, experiment, and design spaces, digital, physical, and everything in between, where people are reminded that God is present in every corner of their lives. It's the challenge and invitation of transforming everyday spaces to places where miracles and divine encounters can happen. It's the beauty of changing common places like the Sea of Galilee to a place where faith is found, shaped, and even where some find new meaning. I imagine those disciples would never be able to look at that familiar place the same ever again. When we approach ministry with intentionality and curiosity, we become co-creators of moments that reach far beyond Sunday mornings and echo throughout people's everyday lives.

Beyond Sunday Reflections

1. Describe your most transformative experiences with God.

2. What are the expected outcomes or behaviors that you hope will be the result of your formation process?

3. Where are people naturally gathering outside of Sunday morning?

4. Discuss the natural rhythms throughout the year, the life of the church, and where experiential learning can be incorporated into the normal practices of people's lives.

Chapter 4

Reaching New People in New Spaces

The church has more tools, more access, and more opportunities to reach people than at any other time in history. There has never been a more ideal time to "go and make disciples of all nations, baptizing them in the name of the Father and of the Son and of the Holy Spirit" (Matt 28:19). And yet, with access to an unlimited number of tools, training, resources, data, and developments, the gap between possibilities and production continues to increase. Mainline denominations are still in steep decline. There will be more churches closed than planted. Aging buildings are still difficult and expensive to maintain. There still exists a decline in religious and denominational affiliations, with a continued rise in the "nones" and "dones." While the pandemic wasn't the cause, it certainly accelerated the trends we now face.

The dominant question many are still asking is, "How do we grow the present and future church?" It's a question that many were asking before the pandemic, and it remains an ongoing mystery that only a select few have managed to solve. This chapter will be dedicated to helping churches not only answer that question in this new context of ministry, but also reflect on the possibilities and barriers that might exist when trying to grow and reach new audiences.

Church Growth in a Hybrid World

Church growth has always been a major focus for ministry leaders, but in today's increasingly hybrid world, where physical and digital experiences intertwine, it's crucial to rethink how we engage with new audiences. Take a moment to consider your *Five Faces*. This entire chapter will center around them. While previous chapters focus more on engagement from the current congregation, this chapter looks outward and considers how we continue growing in a new ministry context. It is our call as a Christian community. It's what Jesus reminded us to do in the Great Commission. It's what Jesus modeled for us when he intentionally made the gospel accessible to those in society who were traditionally excluded.

In the United Methodist Church, our membership vows ask the prospective new members to publicly commit to the United Methodist Church by use of their prayers, presence, gifts, service, and *witness*. While it's an uncomfortable word for some, the word *witness* highlights the evangelistic responsibilities of all members to make their faith "shareable." As we approach the possibilities of reaching new audiences, let's not focus solely on just strategies, principles, and outcomes. Let's also keep at the forefront of our minds the real names and real lives of the people we're called to reach.

As we reflect on the call and desire to connect with our communities, it becomes crucial to identify where a church stands in its lifecycle, so that we can better understand the barriers and opportunities we face in reaching and growing new audiences. As churches find themselves at various stages, understanding where they are helps prioritize the necessary steps for growth and adaptation, especially when confronted with the realities of a rapidly changing cultural and ministry landscape. The following list outlines four possible stages:

1. Turnaround: Prolonged decline marked by noticeable decreases in influence, ministry impact, resources, and capacity. This church is in survival mode.

2. Declining: Steady, often not noticeable or apparent, decline in key metrics such as attendance, engagement, and presence within the community. The past is prime.

3. Plateaued: Growth is stagnant. Maintenance rules. Risks are rarely taken. Church programming has become predictable. No significant progress or decline.

4. Sustained Growth: Growth is consistent and intentional, not just in numbers but also in depth, development, and engagement.

Rethinking Your Reach

Carrying the gospel beyond the walls of the church has always been a challenge, but essential to its mission. History reminds us of its laborious nature. In the New Testament, we witness Paul, the missionary, reaching new audiences by traveling extensively, sometimes at high risk, to major cities across the Roman Empire, planting new faith communities in cultural and trading centers. While he was adequately trained and equipped to speak in synagogues, he also knew when to take advantage of the messages given in marketplaces, homes, and public forums. His journeys brought this new expression of faith from a localized movement to one that spread across an entire region.

Centuries later, we see another reformer, John Wesley, extending the gospel that was just as bold, creative, and deeply contextual. While being excluded from traditional church buildings, he found solace in open fields and tent revivals. He even gathered people in homes and deployed circuit riders across rural America to reach those outside of traditional church contexts. Whether it was Paul's journey to a different city or Wesley's missionary call, each example reminds us that meeting people where they are often requires rethinking where and how we show up.

Recognizing and engaging the places where people naturally gather marks a cultural shift that many churches will need to embrace. Traditionally, church growth methods were centered around *attractional* models. Many of the strategies offered were focused on getting new people to come to a building that held church activities. Worship services were designed for the seeker. Others simply approached it with the expectation that growth would be measured by the number of new people in attendance. Even outreach activities were held with the sole purpose of attracting individuals to a worship service. Therefore, the church's effectiveness and ability to reach the wider community was measured by how many people it was able to convince to "come" to church.

Expanding the reach of your congregation for the future will require a vastly different approach. The differing cultural shifts that we articulated in chapter 1 will impact where people are gathering and the different ways and possibilities of how the church can be present. The goals are the same, but the tools needed to achieve them have dramatically changed. If your community is consistently gathering for worship services on Sunday mornings, this may not apply. However, for many churches and leaders working through this book, most of the people you are trying to reach are not already attending services in the church buildings on Sunday mornings. I would guess that the majority of the people you are trying to reach are online; this is today's largest mission field. Remember, *being* the church is now hybrid. Sunday isn't the only gathering place. With the appropriate use of technology, the church has unlimited access to its community.

As we focus on a hybrid model for church growth, this does not negate the many available options for reaching new audiences. Adding additional campuses or launching new expressions of gathering, such as dinner church, are still valid options for making these connections. However, even with these models, having an active and strategic online presence only enhances these other experiences.

This will require us to redefine or have a fuller definition of what it means to *reach* our community. Reaching encompasses more than just attending a program or worship service. However, a more complete understanding of *reaching* can be defined as cultivating meaningful connections that resonate emotionally, spiritually, and practically. It's when people in your community can look at your congregation and see themselves: their struggles, their stories, their hopes, and their values. *Reaching* is what happens when the community's lived experience is reflected, acknowledged, and understood in the life and direction of the congregation. As my colleagues at Fishhook, a consulting firm that helps re-energize the communication and marketing efforts of the local church, would say, it's showing up in ways that add value;

it's improving their lives. So, how do we continue to help them answer and deal with the urgent and perpetual questions and concerns they are asking? Instead of approaching the idea of *reaching* from an invitation to gather on a specific day of the week, let's approach it with a lens of adding value and improving the quality of their lives.

Work of the Heart

The real question that must be honestly answered before we take a deeper dive into strategy is this: Does your congregation truly have a heart for welcoming, creating space for, and reaching new people? While the question sounds simple, one must not underestimate the harsh reality that some congregations are more comfortable doing ministry with those who are already present. Reaching new people in the community can be intimidating, sometimes uncomfortable, and, often, the cost is too great. It doesn't mean these feelings can't change or evolve; it will, however, impact your flexibility, approach, and your initial commitment.

There are some congregations that express not wanting the church to close or wanting to see the seats full again. Some even lament the fact that younger generations are no longer represented in the church. While these can be strong sentiments and accurate observations, they need not be confused with a commitment or a call to see new people fully engaged in the community of faith. Not wanting a church to die or decline is not a sustainable approach. What happens when the church is no longer in decline? Will you still get excited to leave the ninety-nine or continue evolving? Will you be just as diligent and excited about the presence of new faces when the budget is met and the urgency of sustainability is not being threatened?

When congregations have a heart for their community, their desire is so infused in the life and DNA of the congregation that it becomes the central reason for their gathering and approach to ministry. One of the largest congregations in the United States that continues to plant churches across the country consistently exemplifies this approach. They overtly express this through one of their key values: "We will do anything short of sin to reach people who don't know Christ. To reach people no one is reaching, we'll have to do things no one is doing." Your congregation's desire for growth must eventually be fueled by a deeper call to make disciples as opposed to solving the problems of a shrinking budget or a decline in attendance. You can't hide what's in your heart. Your community will instantly know whether you are being authentic. They can sense where and when they are welcomed. Take a moment to reflect on a few general questions to gauge the level of passion that's guiding your strategy to reach your community.

Checking the Pulse

1. Is your ministry approach generally guided by keeping your current membership connected or engaging new people

2. How often do you take risks to reach those not already present?

3. Do you actively pray for and seek out opportunities to engage with people who are far from God?

4. What is your reputation within your community? Do they have a heart and passion for you?

5. How would you describe your commitment to reflecting the demographics of your local community?

Strategy

Let's make this practical. What's your strategy for reaching new people? Your heart and passions must be aligned with clear decisions and systems that support the desire for growth. If you were to randomly ask three to five people in leadership to describe your strategy for reaching your community, would they be able to immediately and succinctly describe your approach? Would their answers be similar? It's important to remember that simply launching new programs, filling the calendar, or hiring staff to plug ministry gaps are not effective strategies on their own. Churches that are committed to reaching new people make a series of intentional, organizational decisions that support these goals. While there are some outliers to this rule, growth doesn't happen by accident.

Let's rephrase the problem. Instead of asking how you can get them to come to you, reverse the expectation: How can you get the church to them? The question is simply an extension of the Great Commission. How can you continue to live into the promises of a commission that requires the church to go out into the world for the present and the future? Now, if the people you are trying to reach are walking into church buildings looking for connection and meaning every Sunday, then you've solved the riddle. But if you are similar to the 99.9 percent of churches, the people that you are trying to reach are not already connected to your faith community. But they will, if our strategies are aligned with their lived experience.

We are not approaching growth as simply getting those online to return to in-person worship or activities; that is not growth. It's not a commitment to fill the pews again. It's a commitment to matter in the lives of those people not already connected to a community of faith. As you strategically plan for growth, recall that Sunday is not the only day that you have to make meaningful connections with new audiences. Sunday is not the only day that you have an opportunity to deliver a message that speaks directly into their lives and create places of connection and trust building. Your best opportunity at reaching those not already connected to a faith community is not on Sunday morning. Why? Because that's just not where the people you are trying to reach are naturally gathering on a regular basis. Again, is Sunday important? Absolutely! If and when these individuals encounter your worship experience, will it play an important role in their decision to be part of your community? Most certainly. However, on a weekly basis, the people that you are trying to reach are not regularly engaged with you on a Sunday morning; most are oblivious. They attend to their daily lives, wrestling with the joys and concerns of everyday living without ever worrying about your church's song selections. Remember your *Five Faces.* Consider when and where they are naturally gathering. How can you be present and visible in those respective places?

Who's Your Audience?

Your strategy should begin by articulating who you are trying to reach. Don't underestimate the importance of this question. Please don't skip this step. There are countless strategies to connect with new audiences. The goal for church growth isn't just trying to reach any audience, but to develop clear plans to reach your unique community. Before you are invited to articulate the key demographics and values of your intended audience, let's first decide on an essential element of your growth strategy. Are you trying to reach a demographic similar to the kind of people who are already attracted to your congregation? Or are you trying to grow by reaching a demographic that's not already present? Start with identifying the kind of person or demographic that your congregation naturally attracts. (See below for a profile design.) Think about what's already effective and where you're seeing genuine connections being made. If your aim is to engage more of the demographics you're currently reaching, how can you build on and expand the strategies that are already proving successful?

Create a Profile

Age (stay within a range of fifteen years):

Gender identity:

Relationship status:

Age range:

Education:

Income:

Location:

Employment:

Hobbies and interests:

How they communicate and get their information:

Who are their trusted voices of authority?

Important beliefs and values:

Major questions and concerns asked by your target audience

These questions and demographic profile will be helpful regardless of your chosen direction. Reaching new people starts with knowing who they are, what they value, and what matters to them. In many of my consultations and coaching conversations, it is quite common for a church to desire to reach a new demographic that is quite different from the person with whom they generally connect. Normally, it's an older congregation that wants to attract a younger demographic. Or it's a homogeneous congregation that wants to better represent the diversity in their community.

These scenarios highlight instances where a large gap sometimes exists between the demographics of the congregation and those who reside in the community. Churches eventually commit to trying harder at the very things that are possibly repelling their intended audience. Others revert to simply hiring a staff person to oversee a particular ministry that might represent that demographic without having an organizational commitment towards the stated goal. The intended audience has a variety of needs, different questions, and concerns than what your congregation might be accustomed to meeting. Hence, a church will inadvertently design ministries and strategies centered around the people they already have, as opposed to the person they are trying to reach. When this gap in strategy exists, the chances of reaching new audiences and connecting with the community decrease immensely.

Once you have completed one to two profiles that describe the audience you are attempting to reach, now you're ready for the hard part. This will require honest reflection and conversation. Now you must consider the barriers that might exist when trying to reach this demographic. There is a reason that certain groups and demographics are absent from your congregation. Underneath the many reasons is a hard reality that they simply have chosen other places to find belonging and community. There is a reason they didn't add you to their list. If you are wondering why they aren't coming, it's because they don't want to. However, there are always opportunities to rebrand or reintroduce yourself to your community without convincing them to attend an event or worship service.

What Are You Communicating?

It was a normal day. It was muggy. It was uncomfortable. The biblical text lets us know that it was the hottest part of the day. She couldn't avoid going to the well, but didn't want to deal with the judgment or be reminded of her past mistakes and current failures. So, she tried to arrive at a time when no one was around. The plan almost worked until she met a man who knew every detail about her life and had compassion for her. He didn't offer her judgment, but a new life defined by an experience where she would never feel empty again. She was filled with so much joy that the same woman who hid from public shame returned home to tell everyone about the man she had just met. She didn't care what they would say or think. Her story was so compelling that

"Many Samaritans from that city believed in him because of the woman's testimony" (John 4:39). How likely is it that they would have believed if hearing this story required attending a Jewish synagogue? This wasn't just about Jesus meeting one woman at a well, but sharing the presence of God with a community and showing up in a manner that was accessible.

In one of Paul's letters, he asked the question, "How shall they hear?" (Rom 10:14). It's an essential question related to your audience. And yet, it's a strategic question that's often overlooked and undervalued. Growing churches that consistently reach new people have clear and strategic ways of communicating with their audience. Communication matters. What and how you communicate is important. Your target audience will shape how, what, and where you communicate. The age and life stage of your profile will help determine the most effective approach and use of certain platforms. Different generations rely on different modes of communication. Some still rely on bulletins while others use email, social media, text messaging, and other digital platforms. The specifics can be quite cumbersome and overwhelming with the use of such resources as Google Ads, keywords, and target marketing. So, for this section, let's simply focus on the general approach.

The most common mistake made by churches of all sizes is to focus their communications primarily on events and programming. However, in a time when people are already overwhelmed and constantly weighing how they spend their limited availability, church communications must shift from being just a calendar of events. (Most of the events are internal anyway.) When the majority of what the church promotes are programs, services, or ministries, it risks sounding like another item on an already crowded to-do list. If we shift from this approach, we can move from simply *what* is happening to *why* it's happening. What are the underlying commitments that drive your programming? Is it a commitment to a multigenerational community? Is it driven by your church's call to reach diverse families? Is it centered around a vision to see a faith community that welcomes all people? Remember your *why* is just as important as, and in some cases even more so than your *what*.

When churches effectively communicate their why, values, and mission clearly, whether through websites, social media, or even church announcements, they invite their audience into a deeper conversation about what matters and where they may align. When communication aligns with the heart, it becomes a powerful tool for connection and reaching the desired audience in more meaningful ways. Your audience wants to hear about your congregation's impact. They want to know that it's a place with real people with real struggles and real-life experiences. They want to see themselves in your congregation. They want a place to feel safe. They want to be part of something larger than themselves. Much of that is communicated long before they will ever worship in person on a Sunday morning.

What message are you communicating to your audience? Consider and reflect on what you have communicated within the past month. To whom was it directed? Was it mainly internal or external? What values were being expressed? Did you communicate on platforms where your target audience is present, or in ways they could hear? How and what you communicate with your audience matters.

Communication matters, and EVERYTHING communicates.

Who Moved My Pulpit?

While there are many ways of reaching the community through events, outreach, and much more, one of the most effective ways we can achieve this is by *moving our pulpits*. Moving our pulpits is the intentional act of expanding the message and mission of the church beyond the traditional Sunday morning sermon, embracing new platforms, communal and digital, where its meaning can be shared with a wider audience. Traditionally, most sermons die at the benediction. Its shelf life is quite short. While it can have a considerable impact on those who are already gathered, rarely does it ever reach beyond the walls of that local church.

For most pastors, COVID-19 changed our approach to the preaching experience. Our pulpits were moved not by choice, but by necessity. Some had to rethink the location of their pulpits due to technology constraints or methods more user-friendly to the congregation. Depending on the chosen method of communication, some held services over Zoom, Facebook, and even conference calls. For a brief moment, we were no longer consumed with how to get people to come to church. We could not rest on the laurels of our buildings. We had to consider how to get the church to them. We had to move beyond the limited spaces of our pulpits and meet our community in their homes, on their phones, on their car rides, at the gym, or wherever they gathered. We finally could live into the mantra, "meeting people where they are." For the first time, we could not depend on people coming to us; we had to rely on the church going to the people. We had to make the first move.

Some churches completely leaned into this opportunity and moved their pulpits far beyond the confines of their sanctuary. They used this as a chance to not only engage their current congregation, but also to reach people who were not already connected to their faith community. One of the churches I mentioned previously, realized their intended audience had little connection to their church building. Adding another layer to the complexity, they had a substantial online following and multiple campuses. So, they strategically and creatively started to produce experiences related to the themes of their sermon series, moving away from their church building being a major reference point. For example, one series entitled "The Fight of Your Life" was recorded in a boxing ring. Another series centering on themes of wilderness was recorded outside in a wooded area. In another teaching series, they used the pastor's garage as the production site. While every congregation does not have the budget or staff to create similar experiences, it costs nothing to critically consider and strategize around the goal of connecting with new persons using familiar and creative reference points.

I coach pastors, who are natural communicators, to consider other areas where they can transfer those same skills to other platforms. Could they write, host a short series podcast, or schedule an interview with a local community leader? We have reached a critical point when preachers are called to communicate beyond the pulpit. Sunday morning is not the only time the church has to deliver compelling messages.

Consider your audience and the tools we discussed in chapter 1. Are there other areas of connection and platforms that might be available to create content specifically for your target? Discuss how those tools can be used to add value and address some of the questions and concerns people encounter. I'm finding these pulpits can often be more effective when reaching new audiences than the ones to which we have been accustomed.

A pastor in the suburbs of Indiana leads a church that is increasingly committed to inclusivity. During a period of controversial governmental decisions, the pastor responded with a Facebook post that reminded the congregation of the power of hope. As a result, twelve new individuals attended the worship service the following Sunday, drawn by the church's thoughtful and timely response. Furthermore, while working on her next sermon at a nearby coffee shop, the pastor was approached by the owner, who expressed interest in attending the church because of that same post. The cost was minimal, but the impact was significant.

Physical pulpits alone are limiting, not in their power or ability to transform people's lives, but simply in their potential to reach more and different people. Moving our pulpits beyond Sunday is the moment we reclaim our voice in the rhythms of everyday life. This shift gives us more than just a platform; it gives us a presence. It allows us to show up in ways that are accessible to people not already connected to our congregation. By creating content and experiences that add value beyond Sunday morning, churches are better positioned to earn trust over time, increase their relevance, and engage in real time conversations and circumstances as they unfold. Moving the pulpit is a strategic response to the shifting patterns of engagement and places of connection.

1. Builds Trust and Credibility

In today's world, people are bombarded with messages from countless sources: social media influencers, self-help gurus, and political commentators. With so many voices competing for attention, how can the church stand out and build trust? The key lies in consistent engagement and adding value over time, a principle reflected in the marketing industry referred to as the *Law of Seven Touches.* This law suggests that a person needs at least seven interactions with a message before they engage. For the church, trust isn't built through a single sermon or event but through a series of touchpoints that establish credibility over time.

Due to the skepticism that already exists toward religious institutions, trust must be earned gradually through repeated exposure. Just as influencers regularly show up across social media platforms to connect with their audience, so must the church. This doesn't mean just being present on Sundays, but engaging with people consistently throughout the week. Whether through digital content, community events, or outreach programs, each touchpoint strengthens the church's relationship with its audience, making it a trusted voice over time.

As people today curate their "playlist" of trusted voices, turning to different influencers for advice on relationships, finances, health, and more, we too can become a trusted voice when we regularly show up where people are, adding value, and providing relevant, meaningful content. The church can no longer be limited by what happens on one day of the week. Instead, it has the opportunity to be present across multiple platforms, offering a steady stream of support and guidance.

The Law of Seven Touches reminds us that connecting with our audiences and keeping their attention takes time. If the church only connects with people on Sunday, it's unlikely to build the trust necessary to make a lasting impact. In today's noisy world, people are looking for voices they can depend on regularly. However, once established, trust is powerful. At the same time, it requires ongoing effort to maintain. Many churches today face a credibility gap, as they no longer occupy the position of influence they once did. To rebuild trust, the church must go beyond Sunday services, engage through multiple touchpoints, and demonstrate that it's a reliable and relevant voice in people's lives. Over time, this consistent engagement will help the church become a credible voice in a noisy world.

2. Response Time

Sunday comes quick! For those involved in preaching or regular worship planning, the constant cycle of planning and execution can take its toll. However, there are instances when the days seem to linger, and Sunday can't come fast enough. These critical moments are marked by tragedies, celebrations, or the need for urgent responses that often require immediate attention. Many churches traditionally use Sunday morning as the only time to offer a critical response. Depending on the situation, this may even necessitate last-minute changes to the Sunday service or sermon. We know that our silence during these times can be seen as either indifference or, worse, an unwillingness to engage in difficult conversations. Often, there is pressure on the preacher to rewrite the entire sermon to address the urgent needs of the moment. Waiting until Sunday to respond can feel like an eternity.

However, with the proper use of digital tools, churches can have an effective and efficient platform to reach and respond to their community in real time. This allows the conversation to move beyond the pulpit on Sunday morning and engage directly with the needs and questions of the community. That's a gift.

During the pandemic, we sent out daily mobile messages to provide our church community with short, encouraging, and spiritually nourishing content. When Ahmaud Arbery was murdered, I did an impromptu live session on Facebook to share my own experience as an African American male living in a predominantly white community. There was no script; I simply wanted to share my personal perspective as a leader in my church, my community, and my family, and let people hear the concerns and anxieties I was facing. The response from both the church and the community was immediate. Answering these needs doesn't always have to wait for Sunday. You have six other days to respond in real time to real concerns and real issues. Why not use them?

3. Topics

Let's again approach Sunday morning as if it were a numbers game. Let's consider it from a practical standpoint. Even the best preacher or teaching team typically has approximately 52 opportunities each year to address the critical concerns and questions from their community. However, if we account for traditional themes such as Mother's Day, Father's Day, Lent, Easter, Thanksgiving, Advent, Christmas Eve, and potentially a New Year's Eve service, it leaves even fewer opportunities and freedom to address specific concerns facing the congregation and community. Given this limited time frame, the range of topics that can be addressed from the pulpit on a Sunday morning are restrictive. Furthermore, the needs of your congregation may differ significantly from those of the broader community. If there is any diversity within these groups, it's likely that a variety of concerns and questions exist. Unfortunately, it's impossible to cover everything in a single sermon, or even throughout the entire year.

When Sunday is your only platform, it limits the possibilities and potential for reaching new individuals in the community.

While this doesn't mean engagement isn't possible, it does suggest that the likelihood of someone not already connected to faith or a church hearing your message has dramatically diminished. Reflect on your *Five Faces*: Is it more effective to deliver your sermon in its scheduled format this Sunday or to create additional content via an online platform your intended audience is already using?

In fact, the most impactful sermon may occur after the benediction. Here's why: The new people you seek to engage are not necessarily gathering in large numbers in your building on Sunday mornings. That's simply not where they naturally congregate. If we view this as a numbers game, it's essential to think beyond the limited number of Sundays available. The advantage of the digital tools we discussed is that you are no longer restricted to addressing critical concerns and questions solely on Sundays. What you can't fit into a Sunday morning sermon can easily be transformed into other forms of content that may be just as effective, if not more so. The topics that you can now address are limitless!

365 versus 52

When churches embrace these opportunities, it becomes clear that ministry can no longer be confined to 52 Sundays a year. This means engaging the calendar, not just by what happens on Sunday, but how we show up every day. If churches are committed to living out their call to witness and connect with new persons in their community, they must move from a Sunday-centered mindset to a year-round mission. It's a shift from 52 Sundays to 365 days. This is a truer reflection of their lives and their lived experience.

Closing the gap between whom we are already engaging and those in our community with whom we hope to connect is not rooted in our passion, but in our planning. We unintentionally plan to meet in a space where and at a time when they have not scheduled to be in attendance. Sunday morning is not the only way we have to reach new people. However, considering the time and attention it takes to design and execute a worship service every week, it would be unfortunate not to use these hours effectively and efficiently. Sadly, the impact of most worship experiences, including the sermon, ends at the benediction.

Traditionally, churches plan on using a content- or message-related calendar based on 52 Sundays. Normally, when services are planned and orchestrated, the goal centers around the Sunday morning experience. Sermon series are planned, and several of my colleagues plan months in advance. Even the best planners focus their ideas around the themes related to the actual worship service. For example, for those of you who are journeying through this book with a group, reflect on this small example. Considering the upcoming worship service that is being planned, what's your strategy to extend the message you are trying to convey beyond the benediction?

I would recommend adding that component to your worship planning experience. For some, this will be a shift in culture. It will require a different level of thinking and planning. It could alter who helps plan the services and possibly shift the goal of worship. Instead of moving on to another Sunday, you are strategically guiding them to another place of connection or adding value between Sundays. Planning for 365 days looks beyond the centrality of Sunday and looks at every day as an opportunity to provide a touch point during their daily routines and rhythms.

One simple way churches can begin making this shift is by adding an extra step to their regular worship planning process. As you work through the themes for each week or series, ask the simple question: "How can we help people carry the message throughout the week or into their everyday lives?" Refer to the tools listed in chapter 2 and consider the opportunities available to extend the shelf life of the sermon or theme. For example, if you are approaching a series on relationships, what other voices or messages could support the overall theme? Could you host a date night? Could you provide discussions around top-rated TED Talks or podcasts on relationships? Are there articles you could share or create, or books to recommend?

If you are approaching the start of the school year, are there resources for parents you could create, or could you schedule an interview with local school administrators? Could you develop resources for teachers in your community? The key is to think about extending the message and worship experience beyond Sunday morning, in order to reach those who were not present. Consider where people are gathering and how you can show up in those spaces. Start small. This approach will cultivate a discipline of thinking about worship and connection that extends far beyond Sunday mornings.

With so many opportunities to engage beyond Sunday, it's essential to have a clear and intentional plan to reach your target audience. To make the most of these moments, churches need a framework that aligns their content and experiences with the real needs of their community. As planning for engagement beyond Sunday becomes more integrated, consider developing a content calendar. Unlike a traditional ministry schedule, this type of calendar is shaped around the questions, concerns, and rhythms of your audience. Identify the most pressing needs and let those drive what you create. Start small and with something manageable. Even small efforts can add real value and deepen connection. No matter where your church is in its lifecycle, you can engage your community in new and creative ways.

Beyond Sunday Reflections

1. Describe your target audience by using the language and questions provided.

2. Identify who is present in your community but absent from your congregation. Identify the barriers that exist between your congregation and reaching your community.

3. Check your pulse and passion for new people. How might you pray for those in your community whom God is calling you to reach?

4. How might you better position your congregation to reach those not already connected to your congregation? How can you be more present as a trusted voice of authority in the community?

Chapter 5

Getting to "Yes"

Many churches are still struggling to find ways to invite or re-engage others to serve in a time when life feels full and unpredictable. Our new approach to hybrid ministry offers a framework that better aligns with how people conduct their everyday lives. It recognizes that people don't just serve in one place at one designated time. They can serve while they commute, mentor over lunch, organize donations from home, or lead a small group via Zoom. This does not negate the traditional ways that we understand and utilize serving opportunities. None of these conversations is approached with an either/or perspective. Instead, a hybrid ministry approach considers the many different ways that people experience and desire to live out their faith beyond the Sunday morning experience.

Serving in today's context must align with the pace, patterns, and rhythms of real life. One of the greatest challenges facing the church today isn't just declining attendance, but declining participation. Many of the churches l encounter across sizes and denominations share Jesus's sentiments: "The harvest is plentiful, but the laborers are few" (Matt 9:37). So, how do we get them to say "Yes"? How do we increase participation? If the church is truly going to thrive in this new landscape of ministry, we must be open to providing accessible, diverse, and meaningful ways that people can serve and live out their faith.

Vision

"Yes" begins with a vision. If we return to the Sea of Galilee, Jesus didn't initiate a conversation rooted in desperation. He didn't list all the negative consequences that may arise if they were to stay in their boats. He didn't rely on shame or guilt to persuade them to follow. Instead, He gave them a compelling vision, one so powerful that it made them want to drop everything and be a part of what Jesus was doing in the world. This is why visioning is so crucial when inviting people to participate in ministry.

Starting with vision when recruiting volunteers provides purpose, direction, and motivation. It invites people to see themselves as part of something larger—something yet to be fully realized. When volunteers understand how their contributions align with a bigger mission, they are more likely to commit their time and energy. A clear and compelling vision shifts the focus from merely filling gaps to offering meaningful experiences that resonate with their passions and values. This strategic approach ensures that invitations for volunteers' time and efforts are motivated by purpose, not desperation.

Therefore, language matters. Most churches simply ask people to sign up for a task or to fill vacant positions. When this is the common approach, it often becomes just another item on an already congested schedule. When this is the approach, people may prioritize other responsibilities that demand their time and attention.

At the core of every individual is a desire for meaning and purpose. It's an innate yearning to feel that their lives matter. When people can see the possibilities of the future, they're more likely to respond with their hearts, not just their calendars. That's why it's vital to keep the vision consistently in front of your congregation. Share compelling stories of impact and transformation. Let them see the outcomes of their service and commitments.

Some congregations are so intentional about their language that they've stopped using the word *volunteers* altogether. Instead, they use terms like *ministry partners*, *team members*, *servant leaders*, *mission participants*, *ministers*, *skilled servants*, or *difference makers*. While small, this shift changes the paradigm and raises the expectations of responsibilities. The language we use to describe those who serve in the church shapes how people perceive themselves and their role in the larger vision. The right language communicates purpose, belonging, value, and vision. It reminds people that their contributions aren't just helpful, they are essential to the church fulfilling its vision and to their own growth in faith.

Is your vision and invitation compelling enough to motivate people to leave their boats and abandon their busy schedules? One of the fastest-growing churches in New Jersey uses this kind of invitational language: "Want to make an impact? Here's your chance, because this place runs on volunteers. We're talking about big-hearted leaders who aren't afraid to roll up their sleeves and help change the world. Bring clean water to children in Africa. Serve meals to our homeless neighbors in New Jersey. Mentor a middle schooler. Pray for the sick. The world ain't gonna fix itself, so how will you make a difference? Let's get our hands dirty together." This approach creates a sense of urgency and ownership.

People see themselves as part of a larger movement and are motivated to act. How compelling is your church's invitation?

Barriers to "Yes"

Saying "Yes" to serving and participating isn't always as simple as it seems. While many people desire to contribute, there are often unforeseen obstacles that make participation difficult. Remember, these barriers aren't just about willingness; they're also about accessibility, clarity, and the reality of people's lives. Before churches can invite people into meaningful service, they must first recognize and understand the barriers that often exist.

Burnout

Many people are still recovering emotionally, mentally, and physically from the demands of the pandemic, and they are hesitant to take on new responsibilities. The constant cycle of crisis and change left many feeling drained, making the thought of adding one more commitment overwhelming. Without intentional care and encouragement, even those who once served faithfully may be hesitant to reengage. There were several people who needed the rest. They just didn't know how to ask.

Shifting Priorities

The pandemic challenged people to reevaluate their time, commitments, and values, often leading them to focus more on family, rest, or personal development. Many discovered new rhythms that prioritize well-being over busyness, making them less likely to engage in activities that feel like just another obligation. Most churches assumed people would just return to their previous patterns. Now we must connect service opportunities to what matters most in people's lives. If volunteering aligns with their sense of purpose and personal growth, they are far more likely to say "Yes."

Unclear Pathways

Churches often lack clear on-ramps that connect people's skills and passions with real needs. Many willing volunteers simply don't know where to start, whom to contact, or they assume their gifts aren't needed. When serving feels vague, overwhelming, or irrelevant, people are unlikely to step forward. However, churches that provide simple, well-communicated opportunities, along with personal invitations, create an environment where people can say "Yes" with confidence.

Questionable Impact

For years, the church was viewed as the primary location for community involvement and impact. Now people have countless opportunities and options to influence their communities and make a difference, everything from nonprofits to grassroots movements to digital activism. Many who have a heart for service wonder if the church is still the most effective avenue to create meaningful change.

Increased Workload and Life Complexity

Remote work, job changes, parental or caregiving responsibilities, and new routines have created fuller schedules and less margin for serving. While we have expressed this same sentiment throughout each chapter, it's important to note the impact of new routines, especially on church participation. Remember, the increased demands on people's time and attention leave them with little flexibility. Churches need to recognize these shifting demands and offer serving opportunities that fit into the reality of people's lives.

One Size Doesn't Fit All

In today's hybrid world, remember that time is one of the most unpredictable and precious commodities. People are managing full plates. As a result, they accept or decline opportunities with their calendar in mind. The idea that every person can fit their lives into a singular model of church involvement is unrealistic. If the church wants to invite people to meaningful engagement, it must offer diverse pathways to serve. One size no longer fits all.

Individuals have a desire to contribute, but their approach or availability won't always be identical. Some can commit to a weekly role; they will be present and active whenever the church is open. Others may only have the capacity for seasonal or short-term commitments. Some prefer to serve only when it's conducive for the entire family. There are others who are great for last-minute emergencies but can't make any long-term commitments. Some serve in places that are not readily visible to the congregation. Others are interested in exploring ways to serve online.

It's important to recognize and celebrate the variety of ways that people serve within your congregation. At St. Luke's, we have some who serve on a project-to-project basis, while some serve weekly. We have some who only serve when we are conducting funerals, and others who host our online chat every week. We have snowbirds who migrate South when the weather cools, and we have families with very young children. We have members who are local and others who live in different states.

By offering a flexible and responsive approach to serving, churches communicate two things: (1) we see you, and (2) your time and gifts matter. When churches broaden their definition of *service*, they create more opportunities for people to say "Yes," even those whose lives don't fit into traditional volunteer schedules. The goal isn't to get people to fill roles, it's to help people step into purpose. And when people are given the freedom to serve in ways that fit their lives, the impact multiplies for them, for the church, and for the world around them.

Say "No"

A church that regularly says "No" to the right things has a greater chance of receiving a "Yes." Regardless of size, the percentage of those serving will always be smaller than the number attending worship. In smaller churches, this percentage may increase, but the true measure of a church's volunteer health is not just the number of volunteers, but the proportion of those serving relative to the worshiping community.

When considering serving opportunities, it's crucial to assess whether the number of opportunities aligns with the number of volunteers. Many churches express frustration over low participation numbers, but a closer examination often reveals a different issue. The real problem isn't a lack of volunteers, but an abundance of opportunities. Volunteers are being spread too thin across too many programs. This issue is especially apparent post-pandemic, as many churches have yet to modify or reduce programs that no longer serve the same purpose.

If your worship community has been impacted by COVID-19, your church's offerings should reflect these shifts. If hybrid engagement or new attendance patterns have emerged, the church must realign its opportunities accordingly. Volunteers are often stretched across multiple ministries, leading to the perception of a volunteer shortage. However, the issue lies in the excessive number of competing opportunities.

For many churches, cutting or limiting programs feels like a failure, but a clear vision is what makes such decisions possible. Vision helps a church align its mission with its serving opportunities, ensuring that programs reflect the current needs of the community. One of the fastest-growing churches in New Jersey does this well. Despite having multiple campuses, they have simplified serving by clearly listing opportunities for Sunday mornings, during the week, and online. Their global emphasis is singular: providing clean water to the world. This focus channels energy toward one cause, making it easier for people to engage.

Another larger congregation with campuses nationwide also exemplifies this principle. Their serving page lists only ten specific opportunities, clearly defining where they need volunteers. While other opportunities may exist, these ten areas are where they direct those who want to serve. This clarity is the result of strategically saying "No" to other opportunities, allowing them to focus on what's most important.

In many churches, there's an unwritten rule that programs should last a lifetime. However, increasing volunteer engagement often requires a hard "No." Too many programs can spread volunteers too thin. If you analyze your volunteer data, ask yourself: Do you need more volunteers, or do you need to say "No" to certain things so people can more easily say "Yes" to the most important opportunities? Do your current opportunities reflect who you are now, or are they remnants of the church you were before the pandemic?

Saying "No" isn't about doing less, but focusing on what matters most. It's being willing to shift priorities and realign the church's missional goals to meet the evolving needs of the congregation. This approach helps individuals find roles that fit their season of life, schedule, and gifts, enabling them to serve with passion and energy.

Diversity of Gifts

I recognize the sensitive nature of discussing diversity and inclusion within the church, but it is a necessary conversation. The church is meant to reflect the fullness of the body of Christ, as Paul describes in his letter to the Corinthians, where he teaches that "Now there are a variety of gifts, but the same spirit" (1 Cor 12:4). Just as the body is one and has many parts, each with its unique function, so too does the church. Every believer, regardless of background, experience, or abilities, has a vital role to play. By embracing and creating spaces for a variety of gifts and experiences, we honor diversity and allow the church to function as God intended, with each member contributing to its mission.

People are more likely to say "Yes" to serving when they see themselves reflected in the roles and responsibilities being offered. However, many potential volunteers hesitate not because they lack a desire to serve, but uncertainty about where they fit. When asked to step outside their comfort zones or serve ways that are unfamiliar, even the most gifted individuals can feel uncertain. Moses doubted, Paul struggled, and Jonah ran in the opposite direction! It happens to the best of us. What helps people overcome that hesitation is the confidence that who they are matters and their unique perspective, background, and gifts are valued. Especially for those who may not see themselves represented in leadership or ministry roles, knowing they belong can be the difference between reluctance and a passionate "Yes."

People aren't asking if they're good enough; they're wondering if there's space for them to serve as their full, authentic selves. However, when people see others with similar life experiences and abilities using their gifts in the church, it can inspire them to do the same. For example, at St. Luke's, we've intentionally provided serving opportunities for those involved in our Mosaic ministries, which support our neurodivergent and differently abled community. One leader, who uses a wheelchair, regularly serves as a scripture reader during our worship service. Think about the impact this has on others in similar situations. It shows them that their unique gifts have a place within the church and that they, too, can serve in ways that reflect their own experiences.

This inclusivity is critical. Paul reminds us in 1 Corinthians 12:12, "For just as the body is one and has many members, and all the members of that body, though many, are one body, so it is with Christ." This highlights that every part of the body, every person, has a role to play. The goal isn't uniformity but unity in diversity. The church thrives when we recognize and celebrate the variety of gifts within our community, ensuring everyone has the opportunity to contribute, no matter their background, stage of life, or personal circumstances.

As you consider how to invest in the leadership and gifts within your congregation, ask yourself: How can we be more intentional about reflecting the diversity of our community in the leadership we cultivate? Are we creating opportunities for people to serve in ways that align with their unique gifts and experiences? Embracing diversity helps everyone feel valued and empowers them to contribute to the larger mission, ensuring that your church reflects the body of Christ in its fullest sense.

Online Serving

If life is now hybrid, then our serving opportunities should reflect that reality as well. This includes creating spaces where people can participate and make a difference, both in person and online. While this is increasingly necessary, it's also a growing challenge for many congregations. Several churches continue to wrestle with how to integrate online worshippers into meaningful online service opportunities. However, when done intentionally, this approach allows people to live out their faith and make an impact in ways that align with the hybrid nature of modern life.

Churches that have made significant progress in this area have fully integrated the online experience into the overall vision of their congregation. The online community or campus has become a visible and essential part of the life of the church. People recognize its impact not only on the current membership but also on its potential to reach new individuals. By surrounding online ministry with a clear vision and visibility, churches communicate its importance in achieving the broader mission of the congregation. As a result, online serving becomes an inclusive opportunity, inviting everyone, whether they worship online or in person, to participate in meaningful service opportunities.

The key to success is aligning online serving with the congregation's overall direction. If you've made the difficult decision to say "No" to certain areas of ministry, this creates more space for volunteers to explore new opportunities. For example, one pastor has developed a team of volunteers who take the Sunday sermon and create supplementary posts, discussion questions, and additional content to share online. At St. Luke's, we've found success in empowering people to lead online small groups, especially during seasons such as Advent and Lent, when we encourage everyone to participate in a group. Here are a few common ways churches are utilizing online volunteers:

- Online chat hosts

- Prayer teams

- Tech support

- Text encouragement (sending uplifting messages and checking in with members)

- "Share" partners (sharing church content across their own social media platforms)

- Content creation (writers, bloggers, social media posts, short clips, etc.)

- Virtual hospitality (interacting with online attendees)

- Care teams

- Photographers or videographers

- Website design

- Data analysis
- On-screen talent

While this is a new frontier for many churches, it's important to allow yourself the space to experiment, fail, and learn from the experience. The only real mistake we can make is assuming that participation can only happen inside the church building. Embracing the hybrid model means broadening the definition of what it means to serve and encouraging people to participate where they are, online or offline.

Equipping and Training for Ministry

Many churches express a desire to dive more deeply into online ministry and hybrid approaches, but there is often a belief that the necessary skills aren't present within the congregation. While there's some truth to this reality, it doesn't tell the whole story. As ministry continues to evolve, it becomes increasingly important for the church not only to create spaces for people to serve but also to equip them for ministry.

Living in the gap between the church's vision and the existing skills within the congregation can be disheartening. However, this gap doesn't necessarily mean congregations should scale back their dreams. In fact, this gap may serve as an invitation for the church to return to its original call, to equip God's people for the work of ministry. As Paul writes in Ephesians 4:11-12, "The gifts he gave were some would be apostles, some prophets, some evangelists, some pastors and teachers, to equip the saints for the work of ministry, for the building up the body of Christ." This call to equip is essential to the church's mission and serves as the foundation for growing a vibrant, effective ministry. Skills may not always be apparent on the surface, but that doesn't mean they're absent.

Let's revisit the story of Jesus at the Sea of Galilee, where he made critical decisions about recruiting individuals to join him in ministry. Think about the skills these disciples would eventually need. They had to preach and communicate to both small and large crowds, cast out demons, heal the sick, organize communities, and lead with an entrepreneurial approach. They would need to manage conflict, make tough decisions, and lead others through challenging times. These are no small tasks, yet when Jesus called his disciples, he didn't recruit based on resumes or professional experience. If Jesus had been searching for candidates with specific qualifications, most of his disciples would have been disqualified.

Despite the lack of immediate qualifications, Jesus never lessened the vision or demands of his call. Instead, he spent the next three years equipping, training, and preparing his disciples for ministry. He didn't just grow their faith; he intentionally shaped their abilities and provided them with the necessary experiences to perform the essential tasks of ministry. Too often, we ask people to serve without dedicating sufficient time or intentionality to training and equipping them for their roles.

To bridge this gap, it's crucial that churches begin teaching congregants how to approach ministry with a hybrid mindset. For example, we can teach people how to lead effective Zoom classes, communicate effectively both online and in person, or share their faith in diverse formats. We can provide the training needed for individuals to grow in confidence and skill. One of the major reasons why there is a large skill gap is because we, as leaders, haven't taught or invested in training or equipping them. We can't expect people to know how to perform or lead effective ministry in this new landscape unless the church is intentional about identifying the necessary abilities and providing the space for people to learn.

One church has recognized the importance of equipping its volunteers and includes this encouraging reminder when offering their serving opportunities: "And don't worry, we offer specialized training so you can always feel confident each time you serve." This approach to training is invaluable because people are more likely to say "Yes" to serving when they feel prepared and confident. And that confidence is built when the church demonstrates its investment in their growth and development.

The beauty of this approach is that you don't have to start from scratch. Today, there is a wealth of resources such as books, podcasts, TED talks, articles, blogs, and webinars that can be curated to help train your volunteers. And remember, *people learn-on-the-go*! Take advantage of these existing resources and accessibility. Ultimately, equipping and training people for ministry isn't just about building skills; it's about empowering individuals to serve confidently and in alignment with the vision of the church.

Second-Career Volunteers: Embracing New Opportunities for Service

Increasing participation is not always directed at engaging new people or those new to serving. It often involves those actively involved in the life of the church. It's common for church volunteers to serve in specific areas for long periods of time. Regardless of the size of the congregation, people often find certain ministries fulfilling or aligned with their personal interests and, as a result, they stay close to those areas. In fact, I have known people who have dedicated over 30 years to a particular ministry. In some cases, a person becomes so closely associated with a specific ministry that it becomes difficult to imagine them in any other role.

This kind of long-term commitment should be admired and celebrated. Volunteers who serve faithfully for extended periods of time are a vital part of the church community. However, I want to explore the idea of *second-career volunteers*, those who have faithfully served in one ministry area but are now open to learning new skills or taking on new roles that align with a new vision for ministry.

For some, the idea of transitioning to a new area of service may feel like starting over. After investing so much time and energy into one area of ministry, it might feel like a loss. Changing "careers" within the church is challenging, just as it is in any industry. However, much like second-career professionals in other fields, it's not starting from scratch, but starting with valuable experience. These volunteers are already familiar with the church's culture, community, and vision. They bring institutional knowledge, established relationships within the congregation, and a deep understanding of the church's history. In essence, they are beginning with a foundation of experience, not as newcomers.

I've witnessed many colleagues and contemporaries, both in church and secular environments, embracing what could be considered a second career. Some have transitioned out of traditional ministry roles and are now experiencing God in fresh and unique ways. Their ability to adapt to new challenges and acquire new skills has enabled them to thrive in roles that continue to contribute to the broader mission. Others, after spending years in a different field, are now feeling a renewed sense of call to ministry later in their professional journeys. This shift not only broadens their impact but also demonstrates how God can work through a diverse range of experiences and skills, enriching the church's mission in unexpected ways.

Bridging the gap between the skills that exist within your congregation and the evolving vision of the church doesn't rely solely on finding new people. It also includes helping existing volunteers realize and utilize the many other gifts, skills, and abilities they possess, which may have been underutilized in their current roles. It's also focused on providing current volunteers with opportunities to acquire new skills, explore different paths, and contribute to the church in creative ways.

With the abundance of learning tools available today, this concept is not foreign to the current workforce. There are countless opportunities for individuals to complete certifications, courses, and learning modules that help them acquire new skills and adapt to changes in their careers. The same can apply to volunteers in the church. By providing opportunities for volunteers to learn and grow, the church can help its members expand their ministry potential and contribute in new ways, regardless of their previous roles.

Creating a culture of second-career volunteers isn't focused on replacing long-term, faithful servants but seeks to empower them to evolve and take on new challenges that align with the church's changing mission. By valuing and investing in their growth, the church can harness the full range of skills, experiences, and potential within its existing volunteer base.

Everyday Life Is the Mission Field

The church is not the only place impacted by a shortage of volunteers and low participation. My wife and I have three kids who are highly active in sports and other extracurriculars and we experience this often. At the start of many of their seasons, there is frequently a call for more parents to assist with coaching teams, refereeing games, or helping with other administrative responsibilities. On several occasions, there has even been a preemptive apology for the cancellation of a team or game due to a lack of volunteers.

However, I've also seen the powerful impact when the right people step into these roles. On a few occasions, our children have been coached by members who attend St. Luke's. While their participation may not show up in any data report, they were serving a critical need. Consider the impact they had on those children and families every week. They were using their gifts and time to shape the lives of people who may never step inside a church on a Sunday morning. As a former athlete, I can still recall the coaches from my past who played pivotal roles in my faith and adolescent development.

This idea of *serving-on-the-go* emerged as a key theme during our inaugural Leadership Academy at St. Lukes. Originally, the goal was focused on equipping people to lead and serve within the context of church ministry. However, this direction was challenged when one of our participants shared that she was a member of a local school board. Her role impacted thousands of students and their families, and she frequently spoke about how her faith and the values of the church influenced her work. It was yet another example of ministry happening outside the walls of the church—ministry that didn't show up in the church's data system but whose impact was no less valuable.

What if the church intentionally trained, discipled, and mobilized its congregation to go out into the world, equipped with their values and beliefs? The future church must recognize that ministry does not need to happen under the church's name or inside its building. The goal isn't to weaken the church's influence, but to extend it. When people serve in their workplaces, neighborhoods, schools, sports teams, hospitals, or local nonprofits, they are embodying the call to manifest Christ in the world. It's the person who hosts spiritual conversations in their apartment complex or subdivision, without formal church programming. It's the business owner who creates ethical employment practices, becoming a witness to the workplace. It's the parent who starts a support group, the coach who cares, or the school board member who sees the value in every student, teacher, and administrator.

When we release people to serve where they live and work, that's when ministry becomes a movement. In the United Methodist Church, we use the term *extension ministry* to refer to individuals who have been appointed or sent to serve in a ministry context that exists outside of the local church. These individuals serve in various capacities such as hospital or military chaplains, professors, and more. The goal of extension ministry is to recognize and affirm the ministry and responsibility that people have been called to in non-church settings.

Could the church be intentional about equipping people for the work of ministry and deploying them into the community as coaches or school board members? Could we encourage extension ministry with those in the pews? This approach allows for flexibility, enabling people to serve outside the church while also acknowledging and supporting their existing roles. How can we continue to recognize and celebrate the extension ministry that is already happening, and expand it as we help meet the needs in our everyday lives?

When we begin to view our everyday work, interactions, and relationships as opportunities for service, we start to see that the mission field is everywhere. The church's mission isn't confined to Sundays or signups; it's embodied daily through the people who make up the body of Christ—wherever they go, whatever they do, and however they serve. By equipping people to serve in all areas of life, the church empowers its members to live out their calling, making a visible difference in their communities and beyond.

Go

When Jesus gave the Great Commission, he didn't say, "Stay and wait!" He said, "Go." The church's role is to prepare people, all kinds of people, to serve the world as they are going or already gathering: at work, in schools, in neighborhoods, online spaces, backyards, school drop-off lines, sports fields, and band rehearsals. And this even includes the quiet moments of everyday life. This is what it means to "go": To release people into the world with the confidence that their gifts, shaped by faith, can bring transformation wherever they are present.

We are living in a time when serving doesn't have to wait for a signup sheet or a Sunday morning announcement. The hybrid church creates spaces for people to serve in ways that are consistent with their lives and deeply connected to their faith. As leaders and congregations, our role is to make it easy for people to say "Yes" by giving them something meaningful to accomplish and properly equipping them for the work. Don't wait for them to come into the building on a Sunday morning. Go with them into their places of work, their homes, their inboxes, and their living rooms; go with them to their dinner tables or their treadmills; join them on their own timelines. That is how lives are changed, one faithful "Yes" at a time. Our work doesn't stop at the building. God called us to change the world through the power of God's love and the movement of God's people every day, not just on Sundays.

As you have come to the end of this journey, let's pray together:

A Prayer for Every Day

God of every moment,
God of mornings and Mondays,
of laundry rooms and lunch breaks,
of school drop-offs, hard conversations, and unexpected laughter—

You are not confined to one day or one place.
You walk with us in sanctuaries and sidewalks,
in coffee shops and kitchens,
in joy and in the quiet struggles we rarely name.

We confess, God, that we've sometimes waited until Sunday
to expect You, to seek You, to hear from You.
But You've been speaking in sunrises and in silence,
in small acts of kindness, in the messy middle of our weeks.
And so today, we open ourselves—again—
to the sacred truth that You are already here.

Breathe fresh vision into Your church.
Help us to see our communities as sacred ground.
Give us courage to reimagine what it means to serve,

to lead, to teach, and to follow You
in a world that also needs hope Monday through Saturday.

And, so, we ask,
let us be a people of everyday faithfulness.
Not driven by fear or scarcity,
but led by vision, shaped by love,
and filled with the expectation
that You are already at work in places we haven't yet imagined.

This is Your church, and we are Your people.
And may what we create—together—
last longer than the moment,
and carry people through a lifetime,
Not just on Sundays.

Beyond Sunday Reflections

1. What are the major barriers that prevent you or others from participating?

2. Where in your current ministry model are there gaps between people's availability and the opportunities to serve?

3. How might you better equip persons in your congregation to serve?

4. How can you redefine *serving* to help people reimagine how to make a difference in their everyday lives? How can people serve-on-the-go?

Additional Resources Available Online

Take a deeper dive into each chapter of *Not Just Sunday* with practical tools designed to move your church from ideas to implementation. For every chapter, you'll receive a curated set of clarifying questions to guide reflection, promote honest evaluation, and help you apply key concepts in your own ministry setting.

You'll also find targeted assessments—including a Readiness for Change Assessment—to help your leadership team gauge where your congregation stands, what barriers may exist, and what opportunities are ready to be explored. Implementation checklists will help you translate vision into action, while guided leadership team activities will equip your staff, board, and volunteers to move forward together with clarity, purpose, and shared ownership.

Whether you're discerning a new direction or deepening what's already begun, these tools will help your church faithfully engage the other 164 hours of the week.

Scan the QR code below or visit:
https://cokesbury.formtitan.com/ftproject/notjustsunday